FINITE
RESOURCES
AND THE
HUMAN
FUTURE

FINITE RESOURCES AND THE HUMAN FUTURE

EDITED BY IAN G. BARBOUR
CARLETON COLLEGE

ESSAYS BY:

IAN G. BARBOUR
GARRETT HARDIN
KENNETH BOULDING
DONELLA MEADOWS
NORMAN BORLAUG
SENATOR DICK CLARK
RENE DUBOS
ROGER SHINN

AUGSBURG PUBLISHING HOUSE
MINNEAPOLIS, MINNESOTA

Contents

PART TWO: RESOURCES AND GROWTH

EPILOG: VISIONS OF THE FUTURE

1

Introduction

Ian G. Barbour

Global scarcities of energy and food are increasingly evident. Growing populations compete for limited resources. Expanding industries consume raw materials and generate wastes at unprecedented rates. Some scientists and social analysts see only catastrophe ahead if these trends continue. Others find hope in a variety of economic, social, or technological measures.

A series of disasters around the world has made us aware that we face an environmental crisis, an energy crisis, a food crisis, and a population crisis. In the past we have tried to deal with such problems one at a time. Today we realize that world problems are interlocking. When the Arab nations raise the price of oil, it has repercussions for employment in Detroit, strip-mining in Montana, and the production of fertilizer and food in famine-stricken India.

Three of the participants in this symposium were among the first to bring these environmental limits to the attention of the American public. In the early sixties, Garrett Hardin, as an ecologist, was insisting on the finite carrying capacity of the environment and the seriousness of the population explosion. In the mid-sixties, Kenneth Boulding, widely known for his writings in economics, described our global interdependence and the finitude of resources, dramatized in the image of "spaceship earth." In 1972, the first Club of Rome report, *Limits to Growth,* of which Donella Meadows was one of the authors, stirred up heated controversy by its conclusion that population, resource use, and industrial output cannot grow at their present rates for more than a few decades.

Other authors represented here have held out greater hope of extending these limits through improvements in agriculture and technology. Norman Borlaug received the Nobel Peace Prize for his work in developing high-yield grains and new agricultural methods, commonly known as "the Green Revolution." Dick Clark, senior U.S. Senator from Iowa, was a delegate to the United Nations World Food Conference in Rome, and has been active in legislation for increased United States food aid and its use for humanitarian rather than political purposes. René Dubos was co-author of the preparatory volume for the United Nations Environment Conference in Stockholm, and many of his writings have eloquently portrayed the possibilities for creative responses to world-wide environmental and resource problems.

The essays presented here are edited versions of addresses given at Carleton College in Northfield, Minnesota on October 3, 4, 5 and 23, 1975.* The Symposium was partially funded by a grant from the National Endowment for the Humanities in support of Carleton's program in Science, Ethics and Public Policy. Roger Shinn, Professor of Social Ethics at Union Theological Seminary, was asked to comment on the ethical issues raised by other speakers, and to give the sermon at the Chapel

---

*Norman Borlaug was scheduled to take part in the Symposium but was detained at the last minute in Pakistan. Chapter 5 is adapted from the H. K. Hayes Memorial Lecture, given on January 20, 1976, at the University of Minnesota, with the permission of Dr. Borlaug and the Department of Agronomy and Plant Genetics, University of Minnesota. René Dubos spoke on Oct. 23 and thus does not appear on panels with other participants.

service (Chapter 13). The exchanges between the participants were an exciting part of the Symposium, and excerpts from these panels are included as Chapters 4, 7, 9 and 12. The informal style of the spoken word has been retained throughout.

Food, Population, and Development

Part One deals with the problem of food, especially in developing nations. In the 1960s there were high hopes of significant progress in the global fight against hunger. The United Nations called for "A Decade of Development." There were large United States farm surpluses, which were sold or given to food-deficit nations. The Green Revolution, using new high-yield strains of wheat, corn, and rice, together with increased fertilizer, pesticides, and irrigation, brought dramatic increases in crop production in several countries, and great expectations in others.

But then came the series of crises in the 1970s. There were natural catastrophes, bad weather in 1971 and 1972, flooding in Bangladesh and drought in the African Sahel. Ecological overstress, including overgrazing and deforestation, contributed to the famines which occurred in these and other areas. Continuing population growth created an escalating demand for food. There were 75 million more people to feed each year—the equivalent of adding to the globe every three years the entire population of the United States. Following the 1973 oil embargo, there was a fourfold increase in the price of the oil needed to make fertilizer and to provide fuel for farms. Critics began to point to the social and environmental costs of the Green Revolution. Beginning in 1974, most of the United States grain exported was sold to Russia and other industrial nations, helping to offset higher foreign payments for oil, and little of it went for food aid. These disappointed hopes and interlocking crises form the background of Part One.

In the opening essay by Garrett Hardin, two ideas from biology are central: 1) if the carrying capacity of any environment is exceeded, the environment is damaged, often irreversibly, and 2) if limits of growth due to one factor are overcome, another limiting factor comes into play. Man can extend many of these limits by technological improvements, but only with increasing direct and indirect costs. As an example, Hardin traces the consequences of sending food aid to Nepal during the past 25 years. An expanding population in need of more fuel cut trees further and further up the mountain slopes; rapid soil erosion and run-off then diminished the area of productive land, and also resulted in flooding downstream—notably in the 1974 floods in Bangladesh. Hardin concludes that sending food aid to impoverished countries would allow population growth and environmental degradation to continue, so that more people would starve later. Such nations are already like dangerously over-crowded lifeboats; trying to help them would only swamp our own lifeboat. In the long run it would be better for them and for us if we did not send food aid.

In his response, Roger Shinn agrees with Hardin about the urgency of the population and food crises. But he argues that withholding food aid would lead to world unrest and violence which would harm all nations. In an interdependent world, no lifeboat is invulnerable. It would benefit everyone, including ourselves, if we could help developing nations build better lifeboats. He suggests that the prospects for increased agricultural production and population control around the world are not as bleak as Hardin holds. Moreover, our own society is so wasteful of energy, and our food consumption so large compared to most nations, that we could condemn others to starvation only at the cost of our self-respect and human compassion.

Norman Borlaug's chapter outlines the positive potentialities of the Green Revolution in developing nations. The program which he advocates includes: 1) introduction of new high-yield grains, 2) proper use of fertilizer, pesticides, and weed controls, and 3) economic policies to provide adequate funds for agricultural development and stable crop prices. He points out that India and Pakistan more than doubled their wheat production in a seven-year period (1965-1972) and could double it again in the next decade. He makes some interesting observations on the impressive increase in agricultural productivity in the People's Republic of China, which he recently visited. Borlaug is very much aware of the precariousness of present world food supplies and the problems which have arisen since 1972— especially the rise in the price of petroleum for the production of fertilizer, and what he sees as alarmist fears of the use of pesticides. He acknowledges that in the race between food and population, improvements in agriculture will only buy time for birth control measures to be adopted; but he holds that the availability of simple family planning techniques together with an educational program for their use can be effective within the time span which the Green Revolution might provide.

Senator Dick Clark maintains that we clearly have the capacity to bring about significant changes to avert catastrophe; the only question is whether we have the political will to do so. Since half of all grain on the world export market comes from the United States, we have a special responsibility to develop a coherent food policy. The short-term problem is food aid in the face of malnutrition and the threat of famine. Clark describes the legislation he introduced in the United States Senate to ensure that at least 70 percent of food aid goes to countries in real need, rather than being given for primarily political purposes. But he insists that the long-term problem is agricultural development, and here also important legislation has been enacted. For the first time, economic aid has been separated from military aid, and food aid is tied to agricultural research and development assistance. Clark suggests that we should double or triple the appropriations for all these forms of aid. Our total food aid in recent years was less than the cost of one Trident submarine. He holds that population control is absolutely essential, but that birth rates fall largely as a result of economic development. He rejects lifeboat ethics, holding that no country has the right to say that another country should starve, or to decide which people should be written off as hopeless.

Resources and Growth

Part Two deals with the broader, long-range problem of growth—especially industrial growth—in a world of finite resources. Donella Meadows opens it with a discussion of the implications of *Limits to Growth*. A central thesis of that book is similar to Garrett Hardin's first theme: there are delays in biological systems and in social responses which allow population and industrial production to grow beyond carrying capacity—which, once exceeded, would be rapidly eroded. But such "overshoot and collapse" is not inevitable, she maintains, if we act to limit growth. She calls for imaginative thinking about personal and institutional life in a world of selective growth. Small-scale, decentralized technologies would be designed with new goals, including reduction in energy and material consumption and in environmental degradation. New economic structures would also encourage resource conservation rather than labor-saving improvements. New forms of family life might include communal living arrangements in which equipment could be shared. Meadows holds that significant social change starts from individuals and groups, not from national leaders. She practices what she preaches—on a communal farm in New Hampshire.

René Dubos criticizes *Limits to Growth* for paying too much attention to quantitative growth and not enough to qualitative changes and new kinds of growth. "There are no limits to the range of possibilities that are open to the human imagination."

Once we are aware of long-range environmental impacts, we can take steps to prevent them from occurring. As examples, Dubos cites pollution control laws, the cancelling of the United States Supersonic Transport (SST), and the withdrawal of plans to extend Kennedy airport in New York. He is impressed not by the delays but by the rapidity with which social change can occur—e.g., the shift in desired family size in Europe and the United States within ten years, or the transformation of Sweden from a backward agricultural nation to a socially and technologically advanced society in 50 years. He urges us not to think of natural resources as a fixed quantity which is being continually depleted; natural materials continually become "resources" as new technologies for utilizing them are invented. Dubos expresses considerable confidence in the resiliency of biological and social systems, and in man's ability to adapt creatively to changing demands. Human history, he concludes, is a series of responses to new challenges.

Kenneth Boulding believes that though the next hundred years may be difficult, the second hundred are more promising. The future is always uncertain. We cannot predict new knowledge (if we could, we would know it already). Knowledge, along with energy and materials, will be our main limiting factor, but also our source of hope. Learning is the key to the evolutionary future. Boulding proposes four goals in looking toward that future: 1) sustainability (including recycling of resources), 2) the quality of life, 3) population stability, and 4) internationalism with diversity. Politically, the latter would require global institutions, but also regionalism and the decentralization of many functions to avoid the tyranny of conformity. Boulding offers the hope that despite the uncertainties of the future, our actions can be guided by "the vision of a pilgrimage to a better world."

In the Epilog, Roger Shinn considers the sources of the value changes which are required by a world of finite resources.

He notes the contribution of Christendom to the rise of science, but also its failure to prevent the anthropocentric exploitation of nature. A society addicted to continuous growth and wasteful consumption can change only by a fundamental transformation of attitudes and priorities. Moral exhortation alone is ineffective; radical change seldom occurs without external pressures. Perhaps only extensive power blackouts, pollution crises, or price rises and embargoes by resource-producing countries will wake us up. Yet pressures alone may only make the privileged more defensive. The combination of external pressures and a new vision offer some hope of creative change, as the prophets of ancient Israel saw. Shinn suggests that we can both hold up the visions of an alternative future and begin to embody it in our own lives—in new life-styles which will involve sacrifice but also new opportunities for joy, justice, and human fulfillment.

Pessimism vs. Optimism

Looking at the whole symposium, if I were to arrange the participants on a scale from pessimism to optimism, they would run: Hardin, Meadows, Shinn, Boulding, Dubos, Clark, Borlaug. There isn't a super-optimist here—a Buckminster Fuller, let us say, who thinks the globe can support ten times its present population at high standards of living, or a Herman Kahn who argues that the earth has virtually inexhaustible sources of raw materials that can readily be exploited. But such persons are rare these days. Nor, at the opposite extreme, is there here a Robert Heilbroner, who holds that the world is headed for nuclear blackmail, totalitarianism, and a new primitivism.

I am taking "pessimism" and "optimism" to represent a combined estimate of 1) the seriousness and imminence of *global resource scarcities,* 2) the possibilities of *technological solutions* within the framework of existing institutions, and 3) the prospects for needed changes in *social values and institutions.* We should really use three separate scales, since these are three separate questions. Donella Meadows, for instance, takes as dim a view as Garrett Hardin on the first two points, but expresses more hope on the third—and she offers each of us something we can do about it. We should also specify a time frame. Kenneth Boulding is more hopeful about the 200-year than the 100-year prospect, and he expresses considerable confidence in man's technological ingenuity in the long run. Senator Clark, unlike some politicians, is able to think beyond the next election and the boundaries of his constituency, but his frame of reference in time and space is obviously more limited than Boulding's. A legislator, after all, has to focus on achievable next steps rather than distant goals. Roger Shinn sees crises looming and holds out little hope from technological solutions alone, but believes that a combination of severe external pressures and a new vision of alternative patterns of life might bring about value changes and the reordering of individual and national priorities.

How could there be such *disagreements among experts?* Hardin, Borlaug, and Dubos are all eminent scientists, but they differ in their estimates of future agricultural productivity and the prospects for population control. Borlaug thinks crop yields can be doubled and birth rates significantly lowered within a decade; Hardin disagrees. With respect to both food and population there are, of course, major social problems as well as technical scientific ones, and no one can be an expert in all fields. One's field of specialization can also influence one's assumptions. Borlaug, having given most of his life to the Green Revolution and seen some dramatic achievements from it, is understandably hopeful concerning its future contribution. Hardin, having worked extensively with nonhuman populations and ecosystems, is keenly aware of natural limiting factors and of the disruptive impact of human technologies designed to extend these limits. Dubos' estimates are intermediate between Hardin and Borlaug—not unrelated, one might venture, to his stress on man's distinctiveness in nature, and his belief in the resiliency of biological and social systems. In looking at a mixed environmental record in the past, one person can point to the failures, such as deforestation in Nepal, another to the successes, such as the Congressional vote to stop the construction of an American Supersonic Transport (though the Secretary of Transportation has ruled recently that the British and French versions may land in New York and Washington). Without even considering the uncertainties in predicting political and social decisions, there are areas of great scientific uncertainty which one faces in trying to predict the future interactions of complex industrial and biological systems. No one knows whether alternative energy sources, such as practical solar or fusion technologies, will be discovered.

Predictions in the natural and social sciences are influenced not only by uncertainties in data but also by the choice among theories, which express what are taken to be the most significant causal relationships. Theories are commonly derived from conceptual models that selectively portray certain features of the world and assumptions about their interaction. Each of the prevailing resource models seems accurately to represent some situations but not others. The model used by economists directs attention to the role of the market place in resource allocation. When a commodity is scarce, its price rises, which automatically decreases demand and increases supply (by providing incentives for increased production and the development of substitutes or new technologies). The model is useful in predicting short-term adjustments when supply and demand are strongly price-dependent. But it breaks down when demand cannot be reduced by further price rises (e.g., when food is already at a bare subsistence level) or when supply cannot be expanded because a non-renewable resource is nearly exhausted or its environmental costs are prohibitive.

The environmentalist's model, on the other hand, starts from a finite carrying capacity and resource base. Market mechanisms and new technologies can extend somewhat the carrying capacity, but rapidly diminishing returns and increasing environmental costs are encountered. Since the gains expected in agricultural and industrial production are modest, catastrophe can be averted only by strong governmental action to control growth in population and resource consumption. This model seems most relevant globally in considering long time-horizons, or locally in those parts of the world where excessive population is already beginning to produce widespread disruption in natural ecosystems. Neither the economist's nor the environmentalist's model gives prominence to the social, political and ethical problems of widening inequalities in the distribution of food or economic power, within or between nations.

Scientific Data and Value Judgments

Better data and more adequate theories can make the scientific aspects of future forecasts more reliable, though value judgments will influence the assumptions one makes. Values play an even larger role when policy recommendations are proposed, for here there are trade-offs between diverse costs and benefits, and varying priorities among people's goals and objectives. The symposium members differ in their political viewpoints—for example, in their appraisals of the capacity of socialist or capitalist systems to adjust to resource scarcities, the value of diversity within and among nations, or the effects of growing disparities between affluent and poor nations on political stability or revolution. There are also differences evident in the visions of the good life and of the ideal society toward which social change should be directed. Both Shinn and Meadows defend human values and inter-personal relationships which are jeopardized in our high-consumption technological society, and which might be encouraged in alternative life-styles. Another divergence which may be noted is the relative priority assigned to *human freedom;* there are conflicting proposals concerning the forms of persuasion and/or coercion which might be acceptable in order to avoid other threats to human welfare.

Again, the participants vary in the importance they attach to the ideal of *social justice* in the distribution of global resources, quite apart from the pragmatic question of whether growing inequalities would lead to chaos or violence which would harm everyone in an interdependent world. Finally, basic *philosophical and religious assumptions* influence a person's attitudes toward nature and toward technology. Is man to be viewed primarily as part of nature and subject to its constraints, or as the master of nature, bending it to his will—or is there a middle ground between biocentric and anthropocentric extremes? Are man's evolutionary adaptability, social inventiveness, and rational capacities grounds for long-range hope? Or does narrow self-interest tend to blind individuals and groups to the need for more inclusive perspectives? Should past technological successes give us confidence in man's ingenuity at finding creative solutions which cannot be foreseen in advance? Or are the neglected social and environmental costs of technology so great, the interlocking character of world problems so crucial, and the economic and political mechanisms for controlling technology so inadequate that such confidence could be disastrous?

Value judgments as well as scientific judgments are clearly evident in the debate on *lifeboat ethics.* One's choice of a basic metaphor or analogy is likely to be influenced by ethical and political considerations, since any analogy emphasizes some features of a complex situation at the expense of others. I find the analogy of the lifeboat inadequate if not misleading at four crucial points:

1. A lifeboat has a known and fixed carrying capacity which cannot possibly be changed. But the carrying capacity of a na-

tion can be increased by agriculture and technology—though to what extent, and at what human and environmental cost, we do not really know. There is no nation whose situation can be written off as hopeless no matter what is done in the future.

2. Lifeboats are independent and self-sufficient; if one boat sinks, other boats are not affected. But nations are dependent on each other for raw materials, and affluent countries have drawn extensively on the resources of poor countries. The affluent will also be vulnerable if social unrest anywhere leads to domestic and international violence in an age of nuclear proliferation.

3. Lifeboat rations are barely enough for even the most fortunate. But the average American uses five times as much grain as the average Asian or African, and his use of energy and minerals is even more disproportionate. Starvation in one country is less tolerable when there is waste and over-consumption in others, and at least some redistribution is possible.

4. In a lifeboat situation there are only two outcomes. A boat floats or sinks, its occupants live or die—and in either case the problem no longer remains. But a nation does not die and its problems do not disappear. Famine produces not only death but living children brain-damaged by malnutrition. Moreover, in a lifeboat situation, death is the only way to prevent over-crowding, but starvation is not the only means to prevent population growth.

If we are going to use a metaphor, I would find it more appropriate to think of the world as *an ocean liner*. Americans are first-class passengers living in luxury on the top deck, with a crowded hold and an impoverished crew stoking the boilers below. The image of a liner — or, better still, Boulding's "spaceship earth"—would more adequately represent our mutual dependence and our mutual responsibility. The United States imports more than half its supply of 6 of the 13 basic industrial minerals, and we even import many foodstuffs. Of the fish catch in developing nations, only 17 percent goes to feed the protein-deficient local populations; most of the rest goes to make fish meal to fatten cattle in affluent nations. Responses to such inequities are not a matter of charity but of justice in seeking a more equitable distribution, and realism in seeking a stable world.

Similarly, there are value judgments as well as technical issues in any appraisal of *Limits to Growth,* especially in examining the assumptions on which the projections are based and the implications for policy decisions. Did the computer models allow sufficiently for the possibilities of technological improvements in pollution abatement, recycling, and mineral extraction techniques—which might substantially (though not indefinitely) mitigate the contribution of industrial growth to environmental degradation? What would be the effects of no-growth policies on inequalities within our nation and our world? In the past, we have assumed that if the whole pie is growing, even the people with the smallest slices would benefit—without any change in the relative sizes of the slices. Would a steady-state society lead us to take distributional inequalities more seriously? Or would it lead to protracted recession, unemployment and social unrest, with affluent groups or nations hanging onto their power and the poor turning to revolution as the only route to a better life? Can present democratic institutions, tied to elections for short terms by limited constituencies, cope with long-range global planning and action, or are fundamental political changes necessary? How can we weigh the claims of present and future generations, the conflicting demands of globalism and decentralization, the tension between technical expertise and democratic participation, or the trade-offs between individual freedom and distributional justice? These are political and ethical rather than scientific questions.

Donella Meadows maintains that social change must start from the *individual,* and she proposes some alternative life styles which might make sense in a world of finite resources. Dick

Clark emphasizes actions which we could take as a *nation,* and describes legislative action concerning agricultural and economic development as well as food aid. René Dubos portrays environmental concern starting from citizens' groups and spreading to a wider public, to which national leaders will eventually be responsive. Unless you are an extreme pessimist (in which case nothing can avert disaster) or an extreme optimist (in which case nothing is needed from you, since everything will come out all right anyway), you will probably conclude that there is something you can do about it. Perhaps there are creative options for both individuals and nations.

Readers of these chapters must draw their own conclusions concerning priorities and policy choices. Here are some of mine, first about population, then about food, and finally about resources and industrial growth.

Population Policies

I feel greatly indebted to Garrett Hardin for emphasizing the seriousness of population growth, even though I disagree with lifeboat ethics as an acceptable solution. Donella Meadows holds that you should start with yourself; I respect her integrity in deciding not to have any children. But action at national and international levels is also required. Dick Clark speaks of the United Nations Population Conference (Bucharest, 1974) as a significant first step, but its results look miniscule in comparison with the needs. I do not see as great a readiness to act on the population crisis as on crises in food, energy and environment.

At the United Nations Population Conference, delegates from industrial nations talked mainly about the importance of *family planning programs.* Delegates from developing nations, on the other hand, held that *social and economic development* should receive the highest priority, and that birthrates will fall as living standards rise. They argued that it is the industrial nations who are hindering such development by their trade policies and their disproportionate consumption of natural resources. Despite the polarized rhetoric of ideological conflict, each side seems to have learned something from the other. For there is considerable evidence to suggest that *both* development and family planning will be necessary for birthrates to fall.

In the past, birthrates did fall from the process of modernization alone. But industrialization and the "demographic transition" in Europe occurred when populations were smaller, energy was cheap, and the natural resources of other countries were exploited. Overseas colonies provided cheap raw materials for industry, and North America and Australia provided safety valves for population pressure as well as vast new lands for cultivation. Developing countries today have no such advantages. As Peggy Barlett points out in the panel on food and development (Chap. 7), the motivation for large families is largely a product of social and economic forces. One reason that parents in poor countries want many children is that they expect some to die young, and they need several surviving children—especially sons—to work in the fields and to support them in their old age.

The many factors influencing birthrates are difficult to disentangle, but the contributions of *health care, literacy,* and *economic security* are clearly important. In South Korea and Taiwan, the largest rise in living standards and drop in birthrate occurred before family planning programs were launched in 1963. In mainland China, recent visitors report at least minimum levels of food, health care, and education are available to all. The drop in birthrate there seems to be attributable as much to greater economic and social security—and to social pressures for smaller families—as to the provision of birth control services. In India, by contrast, efforts to promote family planning without such social changes have met with little success. Progress in economic development, discussed in the next section, thus appears essential to population stability.

But specific attention to the reduction of family size is also needed. Four aspects of such a program may be mentioned:

1. *Family planning services.* Inexpensive birth-control methodes must be available if the desire for smaller families is to be translated into a lower birthrate. Village clinics can link family planning to maternal health and child care. The United Nations Fund for Population Activities estimates that the cost of family planning services ranges from 50 cents to $1 per capita per year. The two billion people in the less developed countries (excluding China) could *all* receive minimal services for $1 to $2 billion annually.

2. *New social roles for women.* The availability to women of other options besides child-raising can contribute substantially to lowered birthrates. Later marriage, educational opportunities, the opening of varied careers to women, and new identities outside the home can be seen as byproducts of the process of modernization but also as specific goals for social policy.

3. *Economic incentives.* These would go beyond the voluntary measures mentioned so far, but would not involve the degree of coercion some authors advocate (e.g. compulsory sterilization or abortion after the second child). Tax deductions now favor large families; instead, bonuses for small families or for voluntary sterilization could be provided. Such incentives do manipulate human behavior, but with less violation of individual freedom than the alternatives proposed. Provision of even minimal security in old age would also have far-reaching effects.

4. *Education and persuasion.* The line is not easily drawn between education for socially desirable goals and excessive pressures for conformity—which jeopardize human dignity— and the line will vary with the seriousness of the social consequences. A deliberate effort to alter cultural images in order

to legitimize the small family is surely justifiable in the light of the disastrous results of continued population growth. All of these measures, while they seem more urgent in poor nations, are equally important in rich ones. Each child born in the United States will on the average consume as much of the world's resources as 20 children born in India, at current rates.

Food and Development Policies

I am in agreement with Senator Clark that *food aid* should be increased and that its allocation should not be governed by political considerations. Neither pragmatic realism nor ethical idealism allows us to overeat and waste food while others are starving and children are being stunted by malnutrition. Food aid on the scale required can only be provided by national policy decisions. The churches have an excellent record in individual contributions, humanitarian relief, and response to immediate human suffering. They have been less effective in working for changes in public policy and in looking at the long-range causes of hunger. They have encouraged private acts of charity more than public acts of justice.

Reducing our meat consumption would conserve world grain supplies, since it takes ten pounds of grain to make one pound of beef. Ninety percent of the grain used in the United States is fed to cattle. But as Borlaug indicates, most of this is corn, which is not at present a basic human food in most poor countries, and changes in our crop planting or their dietary habits would take time to effect. Affluent nations should indeed reduce wasteful consumption and increase food aid, but long-range action is also necessary. An international grain reserve would provide a buffer against weather fluctuations but would be rapidly depleted in lean years. According to the oft-quoted Chinese proverb, "If you give someone a fish, he will eat for a day; if you teach him to fish, he will eat for the rest of his life."

Our main efforts, then, should be focused on agricultural production in developing nations.

The world is indebted to Norman Borlaug and other scientists who pioneered in the Green Revolution; the extension and implementation of such research deserves major support. The distinctive potentialities of tropical agriculture, which have been neglected in the past, should also be vigorously pursued. But as I see it, Borlaug gives insufficient attention to the social context of agricultural development. The Green Revolution has tended to benefit the large landowner—who can afford the fertilizer, irrigation and other input it requires—at the expense of the small farmer and the landless peasant. There is a danger that confidence in technological solutions will lead to neglect of needed political or social changes.

The 1974 United Nations Food Conference concluded that top priority should be given to *food production among the rural poor of developing nations.* It proposed an increase in international funds for rural development from $1.5 billion in 1974 to $5 billion by 1980—an increase which would be less than 1/70th of current global military spending.* In many countries land reforms are needed if such help is to benefit the poor rather than a privileged elite. Agricultural development occurs within a wider process of development to which we could contribute in three ways:

1. *Development assistance.* Transfers from rich to poor countries will have to be massive if the gap between them is not to continue to grow. Under the Marshall Plan, the United States sent $47 billion (in 1975 dollars) in assistance to postwar Europe. Compare this figure with the total of $5 billion which went to Latin America over a 25-year period. United States development assistance has steadily dropped; in percent of

---

*Documentation for the figures in this section can be found in Arthur Simon, *Bread for the World* (Eerdmans, 1975). For other references cited in the present volume, see "For Further Reading."

GNP contributed, we were 14th among the 17 nations on the Development Assistance Committee in 1974. In some recent years there has actually been a net inflow to the United States when debt repayments are taken into account, quite apart from profits from overseas investments. The Pearson Committee's goal of 1 percent of GNP is a reasonable one, but United States funds for development assistance in 1975 were closer to 0.1 percent. The second Club of Rome report, *Mankind at the Turning Point,* by M. Mesarovic and E. Pestel, concludes that the catastrophes projected by the first report can be averted by sustained development assistance. Their "early action" scenario calls for assistance from all the developed nations starting at $20 billion per year (8 percent of current world military expenditures) and building up to $250 billion by the year 2000. By then no further aid would be needed; the economic take-off point would have been reached in 25 years and further development would be self-sustaining.

2. *International trade.* Trade between nations can also contribute to development, but the terms of agreement have usually been imposed by the nation that is richer and more powerful. An important international objective is the reduction of trade barriers, especially the import quotas and protective tariffs which work to the detriment of developing nations. But, as Roger Shinn says, the narrowing of the gap between rich and poor countries will require not only the "new vision" of international justice and cooperation, but also some "external pressures"—in this case, the increased bargaining power of countries with natural resources in a world of scarcities. The oil embargo may be a preview of what will occur with other raw materials.

3. *Overseas investment.* Are foreign investments beneficial to poor countries, or are they a new form of exploitation and economic colonialism? Many multinational corporations have

financial assets greater than the governments with which they deal, and they can often evade effective regulation by any nation's laws. Without profits there would of course be no investment, but profits have often been excessive, even after allowance for the special risks incurred. The political influence of such corporations on overseas regimes and on United States policy has recently been under investigation by Congress. In the interest of economic stability they have frequently backed repressive governments, allied themselves with privileged elites, and opposed political and economic reforms. But foreign investment in developing countries could be of mutual advantage if directed to real development needs and subjected to stricter international regulation. Provisions for training local managerial leadership, and for gradual transfer to local or national ownership, would prevent the perpetuation of foreign control.

Capital transfers on the scale needed would require a new outlook on international cooperation. They will probably have to be coordinated with reductions in military budgets. If the resources of the world's oceans and seabeds were internationalized, royalties from them could be allocated to developing nations. Research on the distinctive agricultural, environmental and industrial problems of developing nations—which currently receive less than two percent of the world's research funds—should also be greatly increased. The channeling of assistance through international agencies will encourage self-determination by Third World nations in setting their own goals. In some cases, they may seek alternative models of development rather different from the pattern of Western industrial nations. In other cases, movements seeking liberation from domination by foreign corporations or domestic elites will seek a redistribution of wealth and power. Self-determination and human development, as well as agricultural and economic development, are powerful components of the new vision of a possible future.

Resource and Growth Policies

Let us look finally at policies concerning resources and growth. Meadows and Dubos are not as far apart on the issue of growth as one might at first think. Meadows acknowledges the need for industrial growth in poor nations and the desirability of economic growth in rich nations if it is directed to services rather than resource-intensive industries. Dubos has been active in environmental protection and has taken strong stands for energy conservation and against the breeder reactor. But he holds that man's technological ingenuity can extend resource limits further and more rapidly than *Limits to Growth* assumed. He also believes that if the potential impacts of new technologies are anticipated and controlled, considerable industrial growth can occur in the United States without disastrous damage to the environment.

I am inclined to agree with Dubos' estimate of the technological possibilities of United States industrial growth, but I would oppose such growth because of our disproportionate use of resources. Inequities in consumption are a moral rather than a technical issue. The average American uses 150 times as much energy as the average African, and his use of electricity doubles every ten years. Oil saved here can be turned into fertilizer and food in Asia and Africa—if public policies to achieve this goal are adopted. We should not allow the world's remaining oil reserves to be used up on further growth in rich nations, preempting forever their use for industrial development in poor nations. The growth policy which I would support includes:

1. *Selective growth.* Between the options of pro-growth and no-growth lies a policy which asks "Whose growth?" and "What kind of growth?" Global justice requires that future industrial growth occur mainly in developing countries, and that economic growth in developed nations be channeled towards

goods and services (especially the latter) which are not energy-intensive or resource-intensive. The second Club of Rome report (Mesarovic and Pestel) calls for "organic, balanced, differentiated growth" within a framework of international planning. But the pro-growth mentality is so deeply ingrained in American culture that those who favor selective growth will have to devote much of their effort to controlling the demands which the industrial West places on the world's resources.

2. *Technology assessment.* In the past, the developers of most new technologies which promised to be economically profitable were quick to proclaim the direct short-term benefits; only later did the indirect, long-term social costs become evident. The requirement of environmental impact statements on proposed projects was a first step in anticipating such indirect consequences. The Office of Technology Assessment was established by Congress in 1972 to analyze the social as well as environmental consequences of new technologies—before they have acquired a momentum and a vested interest in jobs and plants which would make them difficult to control. There are provisions in the assessment process for participation by diverse groups affected, but there could be more extensive use of adversary proceedings, and input from citizens and public-interest scientists. The criteria for assessments should include public health and safety, environmental impact, energy and resource utilization, and social impact, in addition to direct costs and benefits. If multi-disciplinary assessments are really used by legislators who have decision-making powers, they could significantly influence the directions of future growth. Subsidies and tax incentives, technical standards enforced through the courts, and allocation of the federal research budget provide additional ways of implementing such policy decisions.

3. *Restraint in consumption.* Resource use in industrial nations can be decreased by technical advances in energy efficiency,

waste reclamation, recycling processes, etc. Smaller cars and better public transportation would significantly reduce the drain on
oil and metals. The market-place often enforces some restraint,
as scarcities produce rising prices which curtail demand. But
only a major change in attitudes and values, and a new defini-
tion of the good life, could permanently alter the burden we
place on global resources. We spend $24 billion annually on
advertising, much of which stimulates unnecessary consumption. Perhaps the shift to simpler life-styles must start with
individuals, but a reordering of national priorities and policies
is needed for effective resource conservation.

4. *Intermediate technology.* Without technology, developing
nations will remain in hunger and poverty. Yet large-scale, capi-
tal-intensive, labor-saving technologies are often not within
their reach or appropriate for their situations. E. F. Schumacher's
Small Is Beautiful is cited by several symposium participants for
its portrayal of small-scale technologies directed to basic human
needs such as food, clothing and housing. Production could be
decentralized, using local materials and modifications of traditional methods where possible, whereas large factories tend to
accelerate migration to the cities. Intermediate technology is not
a return to a primitive or pre-scientific society, but rather the application of the best scientific knowledge available, under conditions and towards goals different from those in the industrial West. There are alternative patterns of modernization,
some of which may be less environmentally and socially destructive, and more respectful of the values of traditional societies, than the path we have followed. And small groups are
springing up also in the United States to explore more humane
and ecological technologies. But thus far only a minute fraction
of the world's research funds has gone to such "appropriate
technologies," which represent a less resource-demanding type
of growth.

The Human Future

The future of mankind will be determined not only by finite resources and technological possibilities, but by visions of the future which influence the way people act. The futility of narrow nationalism in an interdependent world may be rationally demonstrable, but people do not act from reason alone. A sustainable and just world requires a global consciousness and an awareness of men's bonds with nature and with each other.

One element in the new global vision is a shift in individual and social attitudes and values. In place of consumption and waste, a new ethic of conservation and careful use of all nonrenewable resources. In place of preoccupation with short-run results, a sense of responsibility to future generations. In place of dreams of unlimited growth as an answer to poverty, a dedication to share existing wealth and to plan for selective growth among those who need it most. The concern for the underprivileged, which has been central in the biblical tradition, is ineffective unless it deals with the structures of economic power which perpetuate extremes of wealth and poverty among individuals and among nations.

Beyond particular policy choices is the need for a new vision of human brotherhood and a new understanding of the nature of human fulfillment in an interdependent world. For Boulding there is hope in the image of human history as a pilgrimage toward a new future. Shinn thinks that attitudes appropriate in facing our future can be symbolized neither by Prometheus, the heroic innovator (who might represent the optimistic aspirations of our recent past), nor by Atlas, the resolute burden-bearer (whom Heilbroner has nominated as a symbol of courage and perseverance in facing the collapse of industrial civilization which he expects). Shinn sees in the figure of Christ the possibility of hope and joy as well as of suffering and sacrifice. It is by such visions of human life and such images of human destiny that our responses to the future are ultimately guided.

PART ONE
FOOD, POPULATION, AND DEVELOPMENT

2

Garrett Hardin

Lifeboat Ethics:
Food and Population

A century ago—even half a century ago—most scientists
would have insisted that science was value free, and that scientists had no business tinkering in anything else. Nowadays I
think a fair share of scientists would disagree with this. They
see that there are values implicit in the practice of science, and
that scientific knowledge has implications for everyday life.
Now my area of competence is biology, and as a biologist, I
think there are many things we have found in biology that have
very deep relevance for human problems, particularly for ethical problems. The concepts I am going to deal with come from
the fields of plant physiology, from ecology, animal husbandry,
and game management. These concepts are rather old; they go
back as far as a century, but I think their implications have not
been pointed out to people. Specifically, the two concepts I want
to discuss are the idea of carrying capacity and the idea of
limiting factors.

Whenever one proposes that some scientific concepts have
meaning for the human situation, one immediately has to be
prepared for a counter-attack that goes along these lines: "These
principles work with plants and animals, but man is more than

an animal; therefore, the principles do not apply." Well, if there is anything that comes out of the last century in biology, it is this: we find more and more that the principles that apply to other animals do indeed apply to man as well. This is not to deny that man is a very special animal. The mere fact of speech at which he is so adept, and all that speech makes possible—a community memory, and the idea of history, and so forth— automatically puts man in a different category from the other animals. So before we get through we will have to see what changes have to be made as we try to apply these concepts to the human situation. But it is important first to see how they apply to the general situation. So let us look at pure biology first.

What do we mean by *the carrying capacity?* If you have a field that has a carrying capacity of 100 cows, you mean that if the farmer is engaged in the business of raising beef and puts 101 cows in that field, he won't make as much profit as with 100. But suppose we look at this from the point of view of the cattle. What does carrying capacity mean then? 101 cows on a field that has a carrying capacity of 100 do not produce as much beef because the cows are thinner. We cannot get inside a cow's head, but I would be willing to bet that the cows in a field that is past its carrying capacity are not living as happy lives as the ones on a less crowded field. On that assumption, we can say that to exceed the carrying capacity is to lessen the value of life for the individuals involved. This has a very real bearing on the famous phrase from Jeremy Bentham, "The greatest good for the greatest number." The exact meaning of that phrase is not clear, but it is often used in the sense that we want both the greatest number and the greatest good. And the whole idea of carrying capacity is that you cannot have both. You can either have the greatest number of cows in the field, or you can have the greatest good for the cows that are there (in other words the maximum health and comfort). There is a trade-off situation—either the greatest number or the greatest good per cow, but not both.

Next, the idea of carrying capacity has built into it the idea of a concern for the future. If you exceed the carrying capacity of a field, not only may you get skinnier cattle, but in their search for food they will trample the ground, damage the soil texture, and preferentially eat up the good plants. As a result of this, rains will do more damage to the soil, there will be erosion, and the following year the carrying capacity of that land will be even less than it was before. So exceeding the carrying capacity not only does damage for the present, it also does damage for the future. If you keep this up, you are constantly robbing posterity of what you might say should be their birthright. And more than that, much of the damage may be irreversible. Now you cannot give any overall statement as to how much is reversible. Some of it is, of course. If soil is lost, you can haul new soil back in; if minerals are lost from the land, you can fertilize with more minerals, and so on. But there are some situations in which the damage is virtually irreversible, particularly on steep hillsides. The damage you do can never be undone—not in historic time, at least, though perhaps in geologic time. So the whole idea of carrying capacity is a posterity-oriented concept.

Now what happens to the idea of carrying capacity when we apply it in the human realm? Several important modifications have to be made. The most obvious one is the existence of science and technological progress. This, incidentally, is the thing that Malthus apparently did not understand at all, living too near the beginning of the industrial scientific revolution. He was assuming a constant carrying capacity forever and ever. But we know that the carrying capacity of the earth has been immensely increased since Malthus' day, and is still being increased. But two questions arise here: Can the increase go on forever or are there limits to growth? And how should we govern our actions in the meantime?

Some people say that we could feed sixteen billion people, or fifty billion people. We could indeed do that, but the question is, at what expense—not only in terms of money but in terms of human effort, human ability and so on? Let me take a particular example. You can produce crops any place on the earth if you try hard enough. But at what expense? In the state of Abu Dhabi, one of the small oil states on the Persian Gulf that has almost nothing but oil and sand, they have set up a system to produce food locally, using greenhouses, complete recycling, distilling water, and so forth—a very fancy system. They're producing crops where the ordinary farmer would say it is utterly impossible. But at what cost? The capital investment in this operation is $120,000 per acre. Even if you could borrow money at 5 percent, the interest on $120,000 would be $6,000 an acre per year. You are going to have to have a very valuable crop to justify $6,000 interest charge per year, and I have said nothing whatever about the operating costs, which are not negligible. So when somebody says, "We can grow crops on the desert," we can agree. We can grow crops at the South Pole, or on top of Mount Everest; we can grow them anywhere. But this is no realistic answer to the food shortage today, and may never be a realistic answer.

Now let me take up the second topic that I mentioned, the topic of *limiting factors*. This is a very simple idea. It was first emphasized by plant physiologists who said that if you have some plants growing in a field, there is always a limiting factor —a factor that is present in limiting quantities which keeps them from growing at the maximum possible rate. If it is iron, and you add iron to the soil, then the plants will grow faster. How much faster? You keep adding iron and finally come to the point when adding more iron doesn't do any good, so then you look for another limiting factor. Maybe it is magnesium. So you add magnesium and they grow still faster, and so on. But at every instant the growth rate of the crop is determined by some factor that is limiting. We can put this in another way. If we increase one factor so that it is no longer limiting, then we necessarily make another factor into a limiting factor. We can never get rid of every limiting factor. So we must ask: "What kind of a limiting factor do we want to live with?"

Let me take an example from recent history to show the great harm that we did by not being aware of the idea of carrying capacity on the one hand, and limiting factors on the other. In Bangladesh in the summer of 1974 there was a flood which covered two thirds of the nation. We do not know how many lives were lost, because the areas in the world where the suffering is greatest are the ones that are under the poorest observation. There were no Western newsmen in the flood in Bangladesh counting corpses. But the Bangladesh government spoke of 10,000 or 20,000 people killed, and this is probably an underestimate. Of course, people are killed not only directly by floods but indirectly by the disruption of agriculture and diseases, and all sorts of other things. So many people were killed in Bangladesh in 1974. The question is, why?

If you go back a quarter of a century, 800 miles from Bangladesh, up in the mountains of the Himalayas, in the beautiful mountain kingdom of Nepal, you get the answer. Beginning after the second World War the Western countries, observing the suffering there—people dying of disease and insufficient food—brought food into Nepal, improved the local food-growing capacity, brought in modern medicine, saved lives, and contributed to the explosive growth of the Nepalese population. And all of this, of course, intending to do good. Saving lives is fine, but one must always ask, "After you've done that, then what? What happens next?"

People also need all sorts of other things—clothing, housing, education, tools, fuel to run the tools, fuel to heat houses, fuel to cook food and so on, and most of these other things can be lumped under the heading of energy. What we did in Nepal was to bring the people food but essentially no energy. So where did they get the rest of their energy? They got it where they always had—from the forests. Cutting forests in Nepal has been going on, and has been doing a certain amount of damage, for a long time. But once the population started increasing, the damage grew exponentially. If you ask a Nepalese how far his grandfather had to go to get trees for fuel, you find he just had to step outside his door. "How far did your father have to go?" "Well, he had a two-hour walk." "How about you?" "Two days." This, in brief, is the story of Nepal. They have had to go farther and farther afield to get their fuel, and they have had to cut the trees from steeper and steeper hillsides.

The results are literally devastating. You fly over Nepal today and you see thousands of acres being ravaged by soil erosion on these steep hillsides that should never have had their trees cut. The soil disappeared so fast that the damage is virtually irreversible. The flooding spoils the terraced farmlands, washing into the streams and going down to the flatlands below. It will plug up irrigation systems, and since without the soil the water runs off the hillside much more rapidly, the peaks of floods are far higher. The floods in Bangladesh in 1974 covered two thirds of the land because of all the deforestation that had taken place in Nepal and adjoining hill country, particularly in the last quarter of a century. So here is the curious situation that we are in; here is the moral challenge we have to face. By saving lives in Nepal for the last quarter of a century, we have destroyed lives in Bangladesh. We have traded lives in one place for lives in another. We can never do merely one thing. Before we ever propose any action at all in this complicated world system, we had better ask, "And then what? What happens next as a result of this well-meant action?"

The greatest difference between the rich and the poor countries is not in the food that they use but in the energy that they use. In terms of food, the rich countries use only about three times as much as the poor countries. That does not mean that they eat three times as many calories, since some of those calories are run through a cow or a pig and converted into animal protein, which wastes some of the calories. But the food production at the primary level (that is, the level of grain) is three times greater for the rich countries than for the poor. But the rich countries use ten times as much energy per person as the poor countries, and there is really the great difference. Or, to put it the other way around, the poor countries are relatively poorer in energy than they are in food.

If we take a barrel of oil as a method of energy measurement —converting coal into oil, wood into oil, hydroelectric power into oil and so on—the poor countries of the world use two barrels of oil per person per year for their energy needs. The rich countries use twenty barrels per person per year. A country like India uses only one barrel of oil per person per year; the United States, sixty. If we make energy the limiting factor—and that is what we do when we send food into a country—then we ensure the pauperization of their life. As the people become more numerous because there is plenty of food, they also become poorer in all those things that require energy, which is virtually everything in life. If they try to hack it out of their environment, we have helped them to destroy their environment more rapidly. And since much of this destruction is irreversible, we ensure that their posterity will have still less to live on. The carrying capacity of Nepal is less now than it was twenty-five years ago; many of the hillsides that used to grow crops no longer can, because of the damage that has been done to them by the erosion coming from still higher hillsides. By trying to save lives, we have lowered the carrying capacity of Nepal.

The moral dilemma that we face is this. If we cannot get rid of every limiting factor, which limiting factor do we want to see in existence in the world? If food is the limiting factor, then people suffer from starvation when they run up against that limit. If energy is the limiting factor, then people suffer energy deprivation which leads them to destroy their environment. Health, of course, used to be limiting, but we pretty well disposed of that when we gained such substantial control over diseases. But we could, if we wished, put disease back in as a limiting factor.

The other important limiting factor that we should seriously consider is freedom, and particularly, of course, freedom to breed. If this is a limiting factor, we have to be resigned to living in a world in which the decision to produce children is not solely a decision of the individual couple or the individual woman, but is in some sense a community decision, and that raises all sorts of problems. I think this is an area that we should take very seriously, admit that we do not like restrictions on our freedom—but then explore the various possible limitations that might be effective if we could accept them. We must ask one by one: "Can we accept this restriction, or could we by some additional engineering make it acceptable?" If we do not accept freedom as the limiting factor, then we are going to have to have one of these others, which are admittedly very unpleasant and which we can hardly see how to make pleasant.

There are two other things I want to say about the idea of carrying capacity. The first is that the carrying capacity for a human population is clearly a function of what we have in mind for the good life. If you want to live a life in which you eat not only vegetables but also have some animal protein, then the carrying capacity of your land is less because there are certain efficiency losses in moving the grain through an animal. If you want to have a life in which you have television cameras and stereo sets and automobiles, then the carrying capacity of your land is still less. So these two things are related to each other in a reciprocal relationship: the higher the standard of living as measured in material terms and in energy terms, the lower the carrying capacity. These are trade-offs. They are matters for justifiable debate. What kind of a life do you want to live? That determines what the carrying capacity of your environment is.

The second point is that the carrying capacity is related in a very subtle way to the actual environment that we live in. Many people have pointed out the interdependence of countries in the world today, and we need to take this seriously. But often this word is used in a very thoughtless way just to put an end to further discussion. I think we had better look at it very closely. When we do we find that though we are all interdependent, the degree of dependence is different between every two countries you can name. Sometimes country A needs country B, but country B may not need country A at all. To make the idea of carrying capacity meaningful in the human situation, we need to distinguish between being self-supporting and being self-sufficient. It's quite clear that no modern industrial country with a high scale of living can possibly be self-sufficient. No country has all of the things that it needs. We need chromium, which we get from Zaire, since there is almost none of it in this country. We need aluminum from bauxite. We have pretty well exhausted our supplies of bauxite, so we have to get them elsewhere—and so on with other minerals. We simply are not self-sufficient, and we become less self-sufficient every day; and this is true of every other country in the world. So how do we live, then? There have to be relations between countries. Isolationism is not possible if you want to enjoy a high level of living in a modern industrial society.

Then the question is, "What shall the relations be?" As I see it there are really only two sorts of relations that are important. One is the relation of mutualism in which there is trade between the countries, a *quid pro quo*—something for something. The other is one of parasitism, in which one country gives and the other country gets. Which should we hold up as a model? It seems to me that there really is no argument about this. A country that cannot be self-sufficient but wants to be self-supporting will be most stable if it exists on a basis of mutualism with other countries—in other words, by trade. If it depends on parasitism, it is not a stable situation and is certainly not good for the receiving country.

Now this brings up the problem of what should we do about all of the desperately poor people in the world today. And this is a terrible problem; no matter what solution you propose, the results are not pleasing.

First, as for the facts. The situation has grown much worse during the last 25 years. A quarter of a century ago about a billion and a half people were malnourished. Now after 25 years of progress, two and a half billion are malnourished. Twenty-five years ago the poor of the world were increasing by one percent a year; now they are increasing typically by three percent a year. So things are getting worse faster. I think it is fitting to remember that this is the centennial of a very famous statement by Karl Marx who said that the ideal state should be governed by the principle: "From each according to his ability, to each according to his needs." Now this is not a completely novel statement. You can find its essence in Christianity and in many other religions. But Marx stated it in such a way as to have a very novel impact. This ringing phrase has stuck in people's minds. Marx himself, I am sure, would have been shocked, considering his view of religion, to have it equated with Christianity. Marx said that Christians say things like this on Sunday and then six days a week live another way. Marx said you should live that way every day of your life. "From each according to his ability, to each according to his needs." Can we live by that philosophy?

We certainly can in certain special situations, such as the family—either the nuclear family or the extended family. I am not saying families do live this way, but I am saying some do, and it *can* be done. You do share in a family in a very real sense, and if somebody needs something, he gets it. But can you extend this from the family to four billion people? In other words, can we take seriously this phrase "the family of man," and run the world on Marxian principles?

I do not think we possibly can because of the ambiguity of that word "need." Who determines what the need is? Does the person determine it himself? Or, is it determined by others? In a family it is determined by some sort of a group consensus. If one person gets a bit selfish, there is a raising of eyebrows, and certain delicate things are said, and presently he knows he is out of line. The family is controlled not by laws but by all these informal control mechanisms, which in a good family work so beautifully that the members are scarcely aware of them. This can happen in a true family; it cannot happen in a "family" of four billion people. If a man in China raises his eyebrows, I couldn't care less. If my wife raises her eyebrows, I shiver. If I am right that a family *can* be run on Marxian principles but four billion people cannot, then there must be a dividing point somewhere between the family and all mankind. This intermediate area, this gray area, is an area that we are going to be studying all the years of our lives.

To what extent should a nation be socialistic and to what extent should it be capitalistic? Different nations have chosen different routes and they keep changing. As fast as we become socialistic, Russia becomes more capitalistic. This is a difficult area, which I am not going to deal with. I am just trying to get across the idea that the world cannot be governed by the principle, "To each according to his needs," because this would be absolutely ruinous. At the present time, if we feed two and a half billion needy people as they would like to be fed, we do a number of very destructive things. As I cited in that example of Nepal—and there are dozens of similar situations that could be cited around the world—if we bring them food only, and no energy, they destroy their environment and make it less able to support their own population.

Of course, you might say we could cure that by sending them food *and* energy. If we want to keep them at the same level of living, that would be two barrels of oil per person per year, and 400 pounds of grain per person per year. Every time we send a ton of grain, we should send ten barrels of oil, or its equivalent in coal or wood. That is a theoretical possibility. But if we wanted to bring India, for example, up to the level of the world average, we would have to send her all the oil that we now import. I submit that this is a theoretical possibility only in the same way that agriculture in Abu Dhabi is a theoretical possibility. I just cannot imagine that we will find it within ourselves to buy all of the oil from the OPEC countries that we do every year, and then send it off to India. And if we did, we know that the following year, since India grows at 2.6 percent per year, we would have to send her the same amount plus 2.6 percent more, and the next year more, and so on. In other words, if you ask "And then what?", you realize that once you embark on this course of action, you are embarked on an utterly destructive course of action—destructive to our economy, destructive also to the economy and independence of the recipient country, and to their environment and the prospects for their posterity.

And yet people say, "But how can you let them starve?" That looks like an innocent question, but I do not think it is so innocent. It implies that there is another option, that we can keep them from starving; and even more, that we are the only ones who can keep them from starving. It seems to me that trying to send food has a very close parallel in the military effort. In the case of the military situation, we once thought we could conquer the world. But after Viet Nam we no longer believe it. We see there *are* limits to what we can do. Yet we still are suffering from the belief that we can save the rest of the world. There is,

I think, a real similarity in pride, in *hubris,* as the Greeks would call it, between the belief that we can conquer the world and the belief that we can save the world.

If you want something less theoretical and more practical, let me point out that during the last twenty-five years, while we have given massive aid to India, we have given no aid to China. What China's situation is we do not know completely, because surely all the first reports cannot be completely true; but even after discounting them as the views of reporters wearing rose-colored glasses, I think it is unquestionable that China is much better off than India. Whatever she has achieved in these last twenty-five years, she achieved without an iota of help from us, and almost none from anybody else. This should make us very dubious of the belief that other countries can be helped only if we help them. It may be that they can be helped only if they help themselves.

All of this is a very hard lesson, and I have taken a considerable amount of abuse for taking this position. And as happens with anybody who does take abuse, I looked around for support elsewhere. I went to the library and looked in the *Encyclopedia of Religion and Ethics* under the subject of charity, and lo and behold I found something that pleased me very much: a statement made by William L. Davidson almost fifty years ago discussing charity. He said, "It confers benefits and it refrains from injury. Hence charity may sometimes assume an austere and even apparently unsympathetic aspect toward its object. When that object's real good cannot be achieved without inflicting pain and suffering, charity does not shrink from the infliction. A sharp distinction must be made between charity and amiability, or good nature, the latter of which is a weakness and may be detrimental to true charity, though it may also be turned to account in its service."

It seems to me that much that passes for charity these days is really merely amiability, in which the people are not considering the question, "And then what?" They are not asking what happens to the land or to posterity, but they just want to be amiable for the present. As I was thinking about this, I ran across some lines written by Stephen Crane in 1899 which I had read as a student in grammar school. Let me read you these five lines from Stephen Crane, and then follow them with some lines of my own that have something to say about carrying capacity as an ethical concept.

> A man said to the universe:
> "Sir, I exist!"
> "However," replied the universe,
> "The fact has not created in me
> A sense of obligation."
>
> —STEPHEN CRANE, 1899.

So spoke the poet, at century's end;
And in those dour days when schools displayed the world,
"Warts and all," to their reluctant learners,
These lines thrust through the layers of wishfulness,
Forming the minds that later found them to be true.

All that is past, now.
Original sin, then mere personal ego,
Open to the shafts of consciousness,
Now flourishes as an ego of the tribe
Whose battle cry (which none dare question) is
"Justice!"—But hear the poet's shade:

A tribe said to the universe,
"Sir, We exist!"
"So I see," said the universe,
"But your multitude creates in me
No feeling of obligation.

"Need creates right, you say? Your need, your right?
Have you forgot we're married?
Humanity and universe—Holy, indissoluble pair!
Nothing you can do escapes my vigilant response.

"Dam my rivers and I'll salt your crops;
Cut my trees and I'll flood your plains.
Kill 'pests' and, by God, you'll get a silent spring!
Go ahead—save every last baby's life!
I'll starve the lot of them later,
When they can savor to the full
The exquisite justice of truth's retribution.
Wrench from my earth those exponential powers
No wobbling Willie should e'er be trusted with:
Do this, and a million masks of envy shall create
A hell of blackmail and tribal wars
From which civilization will never recover.

"Don't speak to me of shortage. My world is vast
And has more than enough—for no more than enough.
There is a shortage of nothing, save will and wisdom;
But there is a longage of people.

"Hubris—that was the Greeks' word for what ails you.
Pride fueled the pyres of tragedy
Which died (some say) with Shakespeare.
O incredible delusion! That potency should have no limits!
'We believe no evil 'til the evil's done'—
Witness the deserts' march across the earth,
Spawned and nourished by men who whine, 'Abnormal
     weather.'
Nearly as absurd as crying, 'Abnormal universe!' . . .
But I suppose you'll be saying that, next."

Ravish capacity: reap consequences.
Man claims the first a duty and call what follows
Tragedy.
Insult—Backlash. Not even the universe can break
This primal link. Who, then, has the power
To put an end to tragedy? Only those who recognize
Hubris in themselves.

—GARRETT HARDIN
(Copyright, 1975)

3

Roger Shinn

Lifeboat Ethics:
A Response

I have certain major agreements with Garrett Hardin that I will indicate briefly, so I can get on to the disagreements which are more interesting. First, I agree heartily on the seriousness of the problem, and I am grateful to him for pointing that out. I think it is immoral to ignore the seriousness or to engage in wishful thinking, as we so often do.

Second, I quite agree that the scientist is not value-free. I do think it is part of the virtue of scientific method that it can isolate certain specific problems and follow the evidence even if it goes counter to the scientist's wish. But the scientist is a human being, and particularly in the application of his findings he works in a social context which affects human beings.

Third, I am grateful for a saying of Hardin's that by this time has become widely known and quoted: "Some problems have no technical solutions." As a theologian I have spent a career trying to point that out. So I should also add, as I am sure he would agree, that there are few ethical problems that do not have technical aspects. To leap to the ethical solution as though the technical issues were not there is foolish. But there are indeed problems that have no technical solutions. Take the very old human problem of not enough food to go around. The problem of distribution is an ethical problem. If you can increase the food rather readily, you have found a technical solution to an ethical problem. And I am glad when that happens, because it is much easier than resolving a conflict of interest. Conflicts of interest are always humanly difficult to deal with. But some problems have no technical solutions, and it is a cop-out to say we do not have to face up to real questions of value. We cannot escape considering our purposes and values by pursuing the mirage of an ideal technical solution.

A fourth point on which I agree is that very often there are clashes of interest. Self-interest and society's interest, or the interests of one society and of the world, do sometimes clash. Not always. Life is not always a zero-sum game, where every win for me is a loss for you. I think a great part of the work of social ethics is to try to transform zero-sum games into positive-sum games; there are often solutions that can be mutually beneficial to all people involved. But having said that, I grant that there are times when there are inescapable clashes. We have to work them through, and social life requires some coercion. And so I quite agree that in some areas of life, to quote another of Hardin's famous slogans, we adopt a policy of "mutual coercion mutually agreed on." Whether I concur in all his uses of that slogan is another question.

Now those are some major agreements, and I hope you see that I mean them. These are not just polite words before one tries to annihilate somebody else, which I do not think I could quite do anyhow. I take them very seriously.

Now my major disagreements. First, on the pragmatic level, I am not at all sure the world is going to tolerate its misery while we thrive in our luxury. We used to think they could not do anything about it. But take just one example—the misery of the Palestinians today. Quite apart from what you want to judge as the rights or wrongs of their situation, they got us involved, and they can make trouble for us. Robert Heilbroner has pointed out how increasingly vulnerable the world is to terrorism. You do not have to be a very rich society to build a nuclear weapon. That does not mean that you can win a war with it; in fact, it is questionable whether anybody can win a war with nuclear weapons. But other people might do us some real harm if they are driven to a point of frustration where they do not much care anymore whether they might get annihilated in annihilating us. So on a hard-nosed pragmatic level I have problems here.

The people outside the lifeboat, to use Hardin's image, can hurt the people in it. They might not just drown passively; they might make a lot of trouble for us. Now, following the image a little further, if it is true we cannot get them all in our lifeboat, we might help them to build additional lifeboats. That might be a better solution than just letting them drown, perhaps taking us down with them. Hardin says, very impressively, that we are not self-sufficient. We have found out that various people in various parts of the world, who we thought could not hurt us very much, can at least cause us major inconvenience, and maybe they can do more than that. That is my disagreement on the pragmatic level.

Second, I would like to go on to a more fundamental ethical level. I see in Hardin's ethic a combination of Hobbes, Bentham and Darwin. I am not saying that is where he got it, but it is all in there. There are worse combinations than that one—but I hope there are better ones. I have some difficulties with his argument, even when it is backed up with a citation from the *Encyclopedia of Religion and Ethics*—a quotation that I never happened on before. I have trouble with the argument about immediate cruelty for the sake of kindness. I do not totally reject that argument; I think at times it is necessary. But I think at times it has been one of the great, powerful sources of harm in the modern world. The Marxist ideology (which I do not dismiss out of hand; I take it seriously at many points) has so often led to the idea, "We will sacrifice a generation for the sake of a future utopia." One never arrives at the future utopia, while the known sacrifice is very obvious. I am not going to push that too far, because Hardin is not promising us a utopia; but he is asking for an immediate harshness for the sake of a future kindness. I might buy that in some cases, but I want to be pretty sure of my grounds when I do it.

And that leads to a further difficulty. Barry Commoner and many others have pointed out, as Hardin himself did, how much higher our rate of consumption is than that of most of the world. The figures he cited on food were about three to one, and energy about ten to one. My students from other parts of the world say, "Such a little bit of retraction on your part could do so very much where we are." That is, if we could withdraw a bit on energy consumption, and knock the ratio down from ten to one, to nine to one, say, that differential could make a great difference in a lot of the world. Not if it were pumped in heedlessly, of course, but if it were part of a sensible plan of development.

Take an example from Lester Brown's book on the hunger problem. He points out that in 1910 in the United States the energy content of the food produced was slightly more than the energy needed to grow, process and transport the food. But by 1970, he says, nearly nine calories went into food production for every one calorie that came out of it. Now this looks like a losing game. (It does not mean that the process is automatically foolish; you are using a non-food form of energy to get food energy, so the energy you get out may be a lot more valuable than the energy put in. But the nine to one ratio is a pretty extravagant one.) Furthermore, we have reached the point where, if you add a ton of fertilizer to agricultural production in this country, you get only two and a half tons, or perhaps five tons, more of crops. But with a ton of fertilizer in some parts of the world, you may be able to get ten, or occasionally even fifteen, tons more of crops. And so when a society is as wasteful as ours, I think we have to be very slow to jump to the conclusion that we cannot do any good for anybody else.

Although I agree on the seriousness of the problem, I am not ready to give up on the solutions. I like what Hardin said about *hubris.* Christian theology has usually called it original sin. What bothers me is that we as a nation—and Hardin pointed this out very well—have so often intervened in other parts of the world to their damage and destruction. Our armies and air force have done it; our CIA has done it on a scale that we scarcely imagined, and for all I know is planning to do more of it. When a society has done that, then to invoke only at the point of food the argument that we really cannot run the world is just too much of a shortcut.

It is possible for societies in great poverty to increase productivity, increase the justice of distribution, increase education, and in the process reduce the birth rate. We have seen this happen in China, Korea, Taiwan, Japan, Hong Kong, Singapore —none of these is an ideal society, but really where is one? They have managed to increase production and reduce the birth rate. I think it can be done. If worse comes to worst, and it becomes obvious that parts of the world cannot survive, I would agree that we want some to survive, and only in that situation— I do not think we are there now—I might reluctantly endorse some of Hardin's proposals.

But who should make these decisions? If I have decided not everybody can survive, and some have to go down the drain, would I ever be willing to say that I would be one of those not to survive? If I am, then I think I would have made an ethical decision. If in every last case I say, "I am going to work this out so that *I* survive and nobody else does," I am not at all sure that it is an ethical decision. And if, for that matter, the issue comes down to sheer power—that is, we have the food, the energy, the military, and the psychic power—if the issue comes down to sheer power, I am not sure we would be the ones to survive. I think Spartans usually beat Athenians in that kind of contest. We are not quite Athenians, but we are certainly not Spartans. And I wonder too what that kind of contest would do to our self-respect. If survival is bought at the cost of the crushing of human compassion, is survival all that worthwhile as a goal?

Let me add a final comment concerning the effects of development and modernization on birth rates. I'm no specialist here, but I think specialists such as Philip Hauser and Roger Revelle have made a pretty strong case, not that increased prosperity of itself reduces birth rates, but that birth rates won't fall except where there is increased prosperity, social justice, and education. Some societies have got the reproduction rate down to close to 2 per woman, but the population is still increasing simply because there are so many women of reproductive age. If you get down to a rate of two and keep this up for a while you'll eventually have a stable population.

I think it is very important to put the data in a context. The sociologists of knowledge have shown us that very rarely are facts transmitted innocently, just for the sake of transmitting facts. They are so often transmitted as part of a world view or an ideological case. Now Garrett Hardin can rightly point out that people interested in development don't usually report their failures. But it can also be pointed out that the opponents of development often don't report the successes; they report only the failures. I've been inundated with literature coming across my desk from right-wing sources recounting all the failures. And the reason they're writing is that they don't want to do anything. And when you don't want to do anything, you report failures. How can you get out of this fix? You can try to get as close to an accurate reporting of reality as you possibly can, but also recognize that biases may be present.

From an ethical viewpoint, I am very much worried that some

of the data we have heard, even if true, are acceptable to us because they take us off the hook. If something's wrong in the world, and I'm pretty comfortable, there is nothing I would rather hear than that I can't do anything, and that various attempts to do something have failed. This is the kind of argument I just leap to buy. But then I realize that we shouldn't buy such a conclusion too fast.

4

Donella Meadows
Malcolm Purvis
Garrett Hardin

Panel
on Food and Population

DONELLA MEADOWS: I have been involved in a number of
world food conferences this year, and in all of them just three
approaches to solving the world food problem are discussed.
One is to do something about population growth; second, do
something about distribution of food; third, do something
about raising more food. Those are really the only three responses possible. The argument seems to be centering on which
is more important: should we worry about population, should
we redistribute the food, or should we raise more food. I do
not understand why we have to do just one of those things;
why can't we do all of them? The problem seems serious
enough to require every response we can think of. Of course
disagreements will arise about how many resources we should
put into each of these three options. It is clear that worldwide
we are putting most resources into raising more food, the technological solution. We give much less attention to redistributing the food, which is the ethical solution, and virtually none
at all on a worldwide basis into doing something about population, the social solution. We hardly even know how to begin
on that one. I would suggest the priorities should be just the

reverse—first population, then redistribution, then increased food production. I think that brings me into very close agreement with Garrett Hardin's position.

However, before we talk about other nations' population, we should remember our own population in the United States is growing. Despite all you hear about ZPG, there are 1.5 million more Americans this year than there were last year, and there will be even more next year, since the fertility in the United States seems to be going up again. The amount of food that the 1.5 million new Americans will eat over their lifetimes is half what the roughly 12 million new Indians will eat over their lifetimes. Our annual new burden on the world's food resources is half that of India's, although they add ten times as many people to the world each year. It seems to me that our first job, before dictating population policy to other countries, is to get our own population under control.

The demographic transition may be of some help to the developing countries, but there are several things working against it. I do believe that if these nations could industrialize, their birth-rates would come down to levels similar to ours. But social changes of that magnitude that affect every family don't occur in less than a generation. Even with the most optimistic assumptions about would population, age structure, and the development plans now visualized, industrialization of the Third World would take several decades, and the result would be 15 billion people in the world. I don't think there are enough resources, energy, capital, and pollution absorption capacity in the world to support 15 billion people living the way Americans live. The demographic transition could happen in theory, but in practice one limit or another is likely to stop industrialization before the transition occurred. Therefore I'm not willing to lean back and let the demographic transition solve all our problems. It may not be able to.

I believe that one of the basic doctrines of all aid programs from the United States should be that death rates cannot be lowered unless birthrates are too. The one thing no country has a right to do is have a high birthrate and low death rate. Any country can settle for high birth and death rates, or low birth and death rates, but there has to be a match. Aid should be directed with that as an ultimate goal. At the same time I don't think that a country which is itself growing at a million and a half persons a year has an ethical right to insist on that position for others. I'm bothered the way Dr. Shinn is, and it seems to me the only solution is to get our own house in order first, before we dictate to the rest of the world.

Suppose we decide as our goal that we will aid countries who are trying to bring their birthrates and death rates into equilibrium. We'll give up our own standard of living to some extent—we will probably have to anyway—and we will bring our own birthrate down so that it matches our death rate. Then what do we do? How do we help? Is what we have done so far in the way of foreign aid productive or counter-productive? I've had to conclude that usually it has been counter-productive, that most of our very well-intentioned help is either negative or harmful in the places where it is directed. One thing we don't really know how to do is to develop another country. A little humility and a sense of mutual experimentation with the people we are trying to help might be in order. It may be that they also have something to teach us. Although we should make resources, talent, technology, whatever we have to offer, available to other countries who need it and who ask for it, perhaps we should consult with them first and find out what they are trying to do. Do they want 18-row harvesters or do they want solar ovens? Big steel mills or tools to cast iron at the village level? E. F. Schumacher's book, *Small Is Beautiful,* describes the possibilities of "intermediate technology," but there has been little funding for such efforts. It seems to me that that's at least a new direction to try.

I would also point out that while we are in the lifeboat with regard to food, we are thrashing in the water with regard to oil, tungsten, tin, copper, aluminum, etc. The list increases day by day because our perceived needs for these materials are growing rapidly and our own supplies are shrinking rapidly. We should keep that in mind while discussing lifeboat policies. You can't really make a food policy any more without also making an energy policy and a materials policy. They have to go together. I suspect that when we finally put them together, we will really understand the meaning of global interdependence.

MALCOLM PURVIS: As an agricultural economist I disagree not so much with the data which Dr. Hardin presented as with the conclusions he draws. When I hear him talking about things like carrying capacity, I have to say that economists have been talking about that for years—two hundred years, actually, since next year will be the bicentennial of the publication of *The Wealth of Nations*. Economists call carrying capacity "diminishing marginal returns." I don't say we have all the solutions, but we have been working on them, and I think we could profitably get together with the biological scientists and talk together about what are clearly common concerns.

We obviously have to be grateful to anybody who has the courage that Dr. Hardin has to think the unthinkable, and to go even further than that, to say it. But thinking the unthinkable does not necessarily mean that you are moving in the right direction. Indeed, there are many scenarios that we could paint of the future of the world, and the lifeboat story is only one of them. I will ask you to think what might be the consequences for our own society if in fact we turn our back on other societies. We live in a finite world, but where are the limits? We would have to recognize that we don't know. But the fact that we don't know where the shore is does not mean that we sound the alarm bell and jump overboard, believing that the ship is about to run on the rocks. There is obviously a capacity beyond which we cannot expand, but we have not reached that point yet.

A publication that was printed in 1925 by a greatly respected agricultural economist in the United States Department of Agriculture came to the conclusion that we could not possibly produce in the entire world more than approximately 12 billion bushels of wheat, and that it would still take us 100 years to reach that point. As it turns out, world production of wheat is almost exactly 12 billion bushels today, and at the same time there has been expansion of many other food grains. The estimates of today's pessimists may similarly be proved false. We should also recognize that science-based agriculture is only 100 years old. This year, in fact, is the 100th anniversary of the founding of the experimental station of the University of Minnesota, along with other experimental stations under the Hatch Act. We still have a tremendous technical capacity that we can put to man's service. We have not yet begun to use what we know about science in most of the developing countries. We know that we have the capacity today to expand agricultural production 3 or 4 times—at a cost and with difficult choices, to be sure, but we do have that possibility. So we do not need to abandon ship yet.

I also object to the ecologist's approach to equilibrium as if it were a perfect state of living. As Professor Boulding has written, what a dreary world it would be if the evolutionary process of man and his society were to stop. Fortunately we have challenges, and food is one of the challenges we face today. It is the kind of challenge to which man has responded in the past, and I think he can do so in the future.

We can take a positive approach to food aid to the developing countries. Nations, unlike individuals, do not disappear; if we deny our abundant food supplies to a country in need, we are going to create additional misery. We will add to the deaths that are already taking place but we will not make the problem just go away, and we might provoke reactions far more serious than we can at present contemplate.

Moreover, we do know something about human behavior, and man's social and economic behavior in particular. We do know that broad based economic growth does seem to lead to reduction in the birth rate—the so-called demographic transition. And therefore we do not have to assume that populations in the developing countries are going to continue to expand. We have to generate such broad based economic growth with high employment so that people can have confidence, security and hope in the future. If we were to provide those things, then many of the reasons for the explosive growth of population might disappear.

What are some of the elements of such a strategy of growth? Clearly it requires the development of agriculture. In agriculture, the input-output relations are subject to all kinds of variability due to weather and things that are not under man's control, and they involve large numbers of people. But a broad based economic development in any country presupposes the growth of agriculture, because most people are working in agriculture. And it's through providing employment that you can provide incomes, so you can raise welfare and provide some stability. If you increase the incomes of the lower masses, about 80 to 85 cents of every dollar would be spent on food. Now suppose that we do have the courage to embark on such a strategy. If you don't provide, in the short run, the food supplies that that demand will generate as employment increases, you will have inflation; and you will have elitist governments who are not concerned with general welfare and economic growth but only with their own welfare.

Food aid can be important in the short run in providing stability and hope. As I said, agriculture is subject to fluctuations due to unpredictable weather. If governments in foreign countries have the courage to pursue long-run strategies, we should give them insurance against such short-run risks. I would agree with Dr. Hardin that food alone is not the means of stabilizing population and redistributing wealth throughout the world. We have to provide more than that. But we have the food, we have the productive agriculture, the resources which can be used today for producing food. I see food aid, then, as contributing to the population control that is so desperately needed. Time is running out. The Green Revolution has only given us a little additional time, maybe a few years, in which to achieve the control of population.

GARRETT HARDIN: First of all, with respect to the high rate of consumption that we have in this country, shouldn't we give up just a little bit to help others? I'm certainly not opposed to that, and I might say that I think we're going to have to do it anyway. As I see it from here on out we are going to be living on a lower energy budget, and we had better learn how to be happy with it. The question is, what happens if we literally give some of our energy to other people? That would buy time for them to work out other solutions. The question is, do we have any way of insuring that they will make use of that time? The generalization that I would put forward is that 99 times out of 100 if a man buys time he throws it away. I think this is what has happened with the Green Revolution and almost everything else; the time is wasted. So don't expect very much from any gifts we might make of energy to other people. But if it makes us feel good to do so, let's do it, but without fooling ourselves about how much good it will do.

I'm glad that mention was made of the necessity of getting other people to take care of themselves, to help them develop technology suitable to their purposes. Here I think there are considerable opportunities and we should make use of them. In general, I think that the sort of thing described in Schumacher's

Small Is Beautiful is really the right approach, and I think we should do all we can to further it. But I would come back again to the issue of *hubris,* of pride. Let's not fool ourselves that we know all the answers. Most of the answers we have given the poor world have not been very good, and we've given them in all innocence. There were economists in the '50s who were saying that the salvation of India lay in mechanizing Indian agriculture. Think where India would be today if they had entirely mechanized their agriculture and gotten rid of all their water buffaloes. With the present price of oil they would be in an impossible situation. Fortunately we did not succeed. Indian agriculture still depends on human muscle power and water buffalo power, and they can get by because they get a lot of miles per gallon out of those two animals. So let's be a bit modest about what we can do.

The same thing is true about agriculture generally. We have a brilliant agricultural accomplishment in our country, but notice that it has taken two or three generations to accomplish. In agriculture it is a long, long way between the dream and the accomplishment. This is partly because of the nature of biology—the many generations that it takes to develop a superior wheat—but it's also the nature of the human animal, and the time it takes him to learn. We have learned about temperate zone agriculture, but we have not learned about tropical zone agriculture. We cannot simply export temperate zone agriculture to the tropics and expect it to work. What we can do is to catalyze the development of similar agricultural experiment stations in the tropics and then wait 20 to 40 years to reap the fruits. This is no short term answer at all, but in a generation or more it should help a great deal. In the meantime we may actually harm them.

Incidentally, on the subject of what we've done in other countries, there is an interesting book, *The Careless Technology,* edited by Farvar and Milton, which is a compendium of horror stories of the results of our well-meant advice to poor countries. The reason you don't hear about this ordinarily is that all of the agencies that give this help have a vested interest in having a good record—government agencies or private foundations— and they're not particularly anxious to hear dissenting voices. And so they do not finance *ex post facto* evaluations of what they've done. The authors of that book have done this all on their own, virtually without foundation support, and have found case after case of disasters brought about by well-meant intervention. I'm not saying we cannot intervene favorably, but I'm saying that it's very difficult and we need to proceed very cautiously. That sort of advice doesn't at all fit the crisis mentality. But I am saying that's all we can do; we cannot meet the crisis. We've got to look beyond the crisis to the day after tomorrow, and proceed very cautiously with interventions.

Let me comment on the demographic transition, the hypothesis that if we make people well-fed and more prosperous, then their rate of reproduction will fall to the point that they'll solve their population problem. I think the evidence for this is very shaky. For example, countries that are commonly cited by Lester Brown and others as examples of success stories are Sri Lanka, China, Barbados, and Taiwan. There are 150 countries, 100 of them are poor, and you can find only about a half dozen that even look like examples of success. Well, the present growth rate in Sri Lanka is 2.2 percent; that means the population is doubling every 32 years. For China, some people give a rate as low as 1.9 percent, others think it may be as high as 2.5 percent, doubling in something like 30 years. Barbados, which only has 200,000 people anyway, does have a very low growth rate, 1.3 percent, but if you look into this you discover it's because the principal export of Barbados is Barbadans to England and Canada. Taiwan's rate is 1.9 percent. There's no question that in some of these countries the growth rate has gone down; it really has. The real question is, how far will it go down? I will grant the hypothesis that if you make people more comfortable, the growth rate will go down. But I would deny that it would go down to zero; in fact, I'd be surprised if it went below one percent. Those figures are for population growth, to be sure, and the fertility rate might be considerably lower. But there is nothing to indicate that people will bring their fertility down to replacement level, which would mean slightly more than two children per woman.

Furthermore in our own country, which presumably is governed by the same principles of human nature, there are some important studies by the economist Richard Easterlin. He has been working with the hypothesis that the number of children a young couple has increases as they have a more optimistic view of their future. From what I know of human nature this makes sense. Using the fine-grain statistics available in the United States, Easterlin shows that you can explain the fall in fertility rate since 1957 precisely by this factor, that the future has looked bleaker every year since 1957 for the youngest of those who are in the breeding ages—the ones who are just starting to form families. Easterlin would predict that if we are indeed coming out of the recession that we're now in, there would be a rise in fertility rate.

You can see the problem. We would like to help people in poor nations by the gentle means of making them prosperous. There are really two weaknesses to this. One is that Easterlin's studies go completely contrary to the demographic transition theory, and I think are far better based. The second thing is that even if the demographic transition theory is true, it would require fantastic investments of capital to bring enough aid to these countries, and to bring education to countries that are 70-95 percent illiterate, and such funds are simply unavailable. It would be about as practical as growing crops in Abu Dhabi.

5

Norman E. Borlaug

The Fight Against Hunger

Let me take you with me on a brief journey to look at the problems of agriculture and food production in relation to world stability and the welfare of man. When we talk about food we first must ask: who produces it? Approximately 50 percent of the current total world population of 4 billion is engaged in farming and animal husbandry. The percentage of the total population engaged in food production varies greatly from country to country as will be pointed out shortly.

When we talk about food we can approach it from three points of view: 1) its biological importance, 2) its economic importance, and 3) its social and political importance.

The significance of food for biological survival should be self-evident, but we seldom think about it in our privileged society because we always have had an abundance of food. During the last 31 years I have had the chance to see things from the viewpoint of food deficit countries. A person can survive only three to eight weeks at the most if he goes into a starvation situation in good physical condition. It is not a pleasant way to die; but beyond that, hunger can be destructive for society as well as for the individual and family.

Second, look at it from an economic standpoint. It was the great production of food during World War II in the United States, Canada, Australia, and Argentina that in large part fed peoples in Europe and parts of Asia when the agriculture of those countries was in great disarray because of the war. After the war we saw an unusually rapid recovery of agriculture, especially in Europe and Japan. This was largely due to the widespread application of science and new technology that had been developed shortly before World War II. I refer to the combined use of high-yielding crops—such as the invention of hybrid corn in which Professor H. K. Hayes played a leading role—better use of the knowledge of soil fertility, extensive use of chemical fertilizers, improved agronomic practices, and better control of weeds, diseases and insects. It was the widespread use of a package of these improved technological practices that led to a rapid increase in food production.

Soon after World War II, production began to soar in Europe, Canada, Australia and in the United States. It resulted in large surpluses in the latter three countries and in Argentina. Our government agricultural policy then was based on: 1) trying to maintain reasonable farm incomes so that especially the small farmers would not be driven off the land into the slums of the cities where they would become unemployed public charges, as happened in the economic depression of the 1930s, and 2) gradually reducing the land area under cultivation to bring production more into line with international market demands. Nevertheless, this policy was widely criticized by the non-rural consumers as being an unjustifiable subsidy to the farmers. We have a unique situation in the United States: in the last few decades much of the population has shifted to the cities so that, according to the last census, only 4½ percent of the people live on the land and produce the food—though by now the figure may be closer to 3½ percent. Today 75 percent of the population lives in large urban areas and another 20 percent in cities of varying sizes. They have lost contact with the soil and with agriculture. They have taken cheap food for granted.

The unique research work that was done in the development of the land grant colleges, university experiment stations, and the U. S. Department of Agriculture has contributed to making technology available to the American farmer which resulted in these very large increases in production.

The non-rural American consumer, however, often fails to recognize his privileged position with respect to food availability and prices. At the end of World War II, the average family in the United States spent about 25 percent of its take-home pay on food. By 1971, with increased wages and lower prices for food, only about 15 percent of take-home pay was spent on food. In developing countries, such as Pakistan, India, or the People's Republic of China, by contrast, about 80 percent of the total population is engaged in agriculture. It is a subsistence agriculture, not very efficient from the standpoint of production of food per cultivated area. In good years Indian consumers frequently spend 75-80 percent of their take-home pay for food. Then when something goes wrong and there are shortages, even though they spend all of their earnings for food they often go hungry.

Third, look at it from the standpoint of social and political stability. When people are hungry, when stomachs are empty, there is social unrest which often becomes social chaos. When such conditions prevail, even though the technology for increasing food production is available, it cannot be applied. Although research can either be done in a nation with a food deficit, or done elsewhere and transplanted or modified to meet local conditions, this requires time; actual food production cannot be changed when political and social chaos reign. When the situation disintegrates to this stage, one will find strong governments of either the right or the left come to power, and personal freedom will be sacrificed until some semblance of order is reached. Only then is there again a chance to try to improve food production. We in the United States take all of these things for granted—including our great personal freedom—and fail to recognize how privileged we are.

Our surpluses of the 1950s and 1960s indirectly and inadvertently contributed to the crisis of the last three or four years in the developing food-deficit nations. Political leaders in those nations had neglected the development and improvement of their own agriculture. The United States would always sell them cheap food on credit; sometimes they received big gifts when there was a crisis. This was a disincentive to the development of local agriculture. Many of the newly independent nations spent most of their development funds on industrialization or anything else except agriculture; yet the largest percentage of their population was engaged in subsistence agriculture. It was really the economies and consumers of the food-deficit industrialized nations of Europe and Japan who benefited most from the 25 years of food surpluses and depressed farm prices in the United States, Canada, Australia, and Argentina; for as their GNP and personal incomes increased greatly, food prices remained very stable.

Our Food Production Base

Now let us ask what it takes to produce food for four billion people. First of all we must look at the land we have to deal with. We get the impression that this is a big globe, yet if we go out on a clear night and look up into the heavens, we have a feeling that this planet Earth is an insignificant speck in the total universe. Approximately 72 percent of the earth's surface is covered by water. Nevertheless, most of our food is produced on the land. Only about 70 million tons of fish and marine products are harvested annually. Much of the 28 percent of the earth's surface that is land is poor real estate. Only about 11 percent of the land is classed as arable, but some of the classifications are dubious. In land reforms in many parts of the world, I have seen land being passed out to peasant farmers which is incapable of producing enough food for grasshoppers in any numbers, much less for people. Often it is completely worthless, but classified as arable land for political reasons. So be careful about accepting the figures that I am going to present; don't take them as more than a very general indication.

Eleven percent of the land area is classed as arable or permanent crop land, including permanent tree crops such as coffee, tea, fruits, and nuts. There is about twice that much in meadows and pasture land, which brings the total to 33 percent. Then there is about 30 percent that is called forest land, but be careful again; some of it may have a few miserable juniper trees in the middle of vast tracts of sagebrush. That would bring us up to 63 percent. Most of the rest is essentially useless: arctic tundra, wasteland under ice in Antarctica and parts of the Arctic, or deserts where water is the limiting factor. Then there are rocky outcroppings and mountainous areas without any soil on them. Much land that was valuable for agriculture has been covered by cities, housing developments, industries, roads, highways, airports, and so forth. Currently, in the United States alone, we are annually removing between 2 and 3 million acres, frequently from our best crop land, for these uses. The truth is that the United States, even now, has no land use policy.

The world is running short of land for food production. Many of the most populous countries of the world have little or no unused land that can be rapidly opened to cultivation. It is true that there are still some countries in the world where there is land that can be opened to cultivation. Brazil is one— it has vast tracts of land with good rainfall. Despite the fact that 25 years ago lands known as Campo Cerrado were classified as worthless because they are heavily leached of nutrients and highly acid, these lands in recent years have been responsible for most of the big jump in Brazilian soybean production. Soybean production has increased from 350,000 metric tons in 1965 to approximately 10 million tons in 1975.

Since the first recorded history there have been many crises in food production and famines, whether caused by droughts or plant diseases or hordes of locusts. After each crisis, more land was opened to cultivation—for land was plentiful—to feed the growing populations. But the population growth in those early times was slow because man had little control over either the environment, his food supply, or his own diseases. This year we are celebrating 200 years since the birth of this country; our lands were opened largely during that time. How much more land can we and the rest of the world open in the next 200 years? In many countries, especially where yields are still low and where population density is great, there is little additional land that can be cultivated; most of the increase in food production will consequently have to be achieved by the development and application of science and technology to increase food production per acre. We have done this successfully in the United States largely through the development of research in land grant colleges, the agricultural experiment stations, the Department of Agriculture, and more recently by research in the agro-industries. This new information and technology has been adapted and put into production by the American farmer and livestock producer to greatly increase food production. Much of the rest of the world has not had this same good fortune. The problem then is to help them in the years ahead to rapidly improve their yields. There are various agencies that have been trying to do this in the last two decades with at best only modest success. All too often their approach in the past has been too academic, too abstract—counseling and advising from the comforts of the capital cities rather than entering into the production fray in the mud, dust, and sweat on the farms in the rural areas where the food is produced. The extension approach used with great success in the United States—with its well-educated, sophisticated farmers—is ineffective elsewhere. We will have to be more efficient in both our research, extension and educational assistance in the future if we are going to avoid even more chaos than we have experienced recently.

Cereal Requirements for Four Billion People

It takes a lot of food to feed four billion people. Suppose we use as a yardstick the amount of cereal grains that was produced in 1971, which was a world record crop up to that time. I do not wish to imply that other foods such as potatoes, yams, cassava, sugar, beans, peas, lentils, chickpeas, cowpeas, soybeans and other oilseeds, fruits, vegetables and nuts, forages, meats, milk, eggs, and fish are not important. But cereal grains provide a good indicator of world food production because they are grown on about 50 percent of the total cultivated land area, and they supply directly about 52 percent of the total calorie intake, and almost 50 percent of the total protein intake. Indirectly they are also fed to animals to produce much of our meat, eggs and milk. By cereal grains I mean all of them collectively: wheat, oats, corn, rye, barley, rice, sorghum, millet, etc.

The total world production of cereal grains in 1971 was approximately 1.2 billion metric tons. In bushel equivalents, it would be roughly 44 billion bushels. Most of us cannot visualize such figures. So let us imagine it as a highway of grain all the way around the earth at the equator, 55 feet in width and 6 feet in depth. That is the amount of grain we produced in 1971. But since there are 80 million more people each year, if we are going to supply the same amount per capita we will have to increase cereal grain production each year by 2 percent, and then add another one-half percent to account for more affluent eating habits including more meat—or by a total of 30 million tons more annually. This 2½ percent annual increase could be represented by the need to extend the highway of grain, 55 feet wide and 6 feet deep, by 625 miles a year—just to maintain our present per capita food consumption.

In 1972 there were severe crop failures in the Soviet Union, across South Asia, and in the Sahel countries of Africa, primarily because of drought. Consequently it was not possible to build that new stretch of the grain highway from current production; we took the grain from stocks and warehouses instead. That was the same reserve we had cursed our government for permitting to accumulate in the 1960s. As the grain stocks were sharply reduced, the economic law of supply and demand began to operate once again. Reserves dropped to a critical level and prices of grain and meat started to skyrocket. Then the American people suddenly found out that food was important. There were great outcries against the farmer fleecing the poor urban consumer and against anyone who was involved in the sale of grain. The large grain sales by Canada, the United States, and Australia to Russia were made very rapidly and no one had any inkling of the magnitude of the Russian deficit—the Russians were good poker players. They had not divulged many of the facts which we insist on having spread across the pages of a free press. I don't think there was any skulduggery on the part of the Department of Agriculture or our government officials. But we found out that the Communist nations know how to deal also in a capitalist style, and they out-dealt us. So the prices of food started to soar. And to their consternation many Americans found out that food doesn't grow in the supermarkets and that agriculture is of some importance.

In 1973 we were more or less on target in cereal production but could not put anything back into reserve stocks. Then came 1974, and again no reserve was built up. We had great expectations in early 1974, but they remained only expectations that never became production realities. First in the spring there were unusually heavy rains and floods, and farmers could not get into the fields; this was followed by a drought of about 60 days, and we finished the season with an early frost. Despite the fact that we had put back into production the 50 million acres of land that had been taken out in the period of surpluses during the 1960s, we added nothing to the dwindling world grain reserves. This points up how land in reserve is not necessarily food in the warehouse. It is like copper in an underground vein—not in ingots.

In 1975 there were good crops generally around the world with the exception of the Soviet Union, which programmed for 215 million metric tons of grain but appears to have harvested only about 140 million tons. Their deficit is much bigger than in 1972; much of their livestock is being slaughtered and they will cut back on grain imports as far as they can. So consequently, again in 1975-76, there has not been and will not be any building up of reserve grain stocks on a world-wide basis. Nevertheless, the situation has eased temporarily in the developing nations because of good 1975 crops.

Energy and Food Production

Right in the middle of the grain shortages in 1973 there were big changes in oil prices by the OPEC nations, which affected not only the supply of energy, but also fertilizer production. What could the developing nations do? Agriculture is an ancient profession in most of those nations; the land has been farmed for hundreds and even thousands of years in some cases. Conventional farming has often been a mining operation, removing plant nutrients and putting little or nothing back into the soil. The grain is used for human consumption and the straw is frequently the only feed for bullocks, oxen, and buffalo. The cow dung becomes the fuel to cook food, because the forests have long since been cut down in many of these densely populated lands. So no nutrients are returned to the soil.

Today one sometimes hears organic food gardeners and food faddists say that if we just used organic farming methods we could produce all of the food the world requires and achieve this without using expensive and unnecessary chemical fertilizer. One can only reply that organic gardening methods are wonderful for growing six highly productive tomato plants and ten lovely rose bushes in one's backyard, but completely inadequate for restoring fertility to worn-out soils on farms required to produce the food for four billion people. In the first place, the amount of organic manures available to meet the world needs is completely inadequate; and in the second place, the costs of shipment of organic manures would be prohibitive were it available. Dry cattle dung, excellent for organic gardening, sells in small plastic bags in eastern cities on a pound for pound basis at more than double the price of pasteurized milk.

There are those poorly informed individuals who seem to question whether agriculture can justifiably continue to use scarce fossil fuel for the production of chemical fertilizer. They ask whether good plant breeders can't produce varieties of crop plants that are capable of producing high grain yields even when grown on nutrient-deficient impoverished soils, without the use of chemical fertilizer. My only reply is that we will succeed in producing such varieties of crop plants about six months after some political leaders, sociologists, and economists produce a new race of man that needs no food in order to grow, maintain health, work effectively, enjoy life and talk eloquently. Often these individuals seem to be the same utopians that curse plant breeders for having been unable to produce a variety of grain that will grow well and produce high yields on small farms but yield poorly when grown with the same technology on large farms. Unfortunately this has been unachievable because plant varieties are both apolitical and impersonal.

What about the use of fossil fuels for the production of chemical fertilizer? When I was in Saudi Arabia recently, I read about 6 billion cubic feet of gas being flared each day from wellheads and refineries in that country. The gas flared in that one country alone would supply the energy and raw materials for one hundred fifty-seven 1,000-ton-a-day anhydrous ammonia fertilizer plants, which is enough to produce 45 million tons of nitrogen annually—more than the whole world uses as fertilizer at the present time. And vast quantities of gas are also being flared in perhaps 20 other countries. It should be indicated that nitrogenous fertilizer can also be produced efficiently from coal when the need arises.

One now frequently hears that mechanized modern agriculture is too energy intensive and requires vast quantities of scarce fossil fuel. Do we want American farmers to go back to the good old days of four-legged horse power, or even back farther to the drudgery of human muscle power? Why not go back to the cheapest of all, human slave power? When one hears or reads such nonsense in publications issuing from our universities, one has to be concerned about what is happening to our common sense. Have we lost touch with the farmer and his problems? The truth of the matter is that the energy used in food production on American farms represents somewhere between 1.3 and 2.6 percent of the total national energy budget, depending on how the calculations are made. When one considers the energy used on food from the farm gate through processing to your table, inputs in transportation, refrigeration, distribution and preparation, the total mounts greatly. Of course our whole transport system is the portion of the chain that really guzzles fossil fuel. It is convenient, but anything but efficient.

The Good Old Days Before Pest Control Chemicals

Today there are many in the environmental movement that apparently believe that modern science and technology are the real cause of our weed, insect and disease problems that threaten our crops and forests. They seem to feel that before the advent of agricultural chemicals—and especially pesticides—nature maintained a biological balance that prevented serious crop losses. Of course this is not so, for the earliest historical records, beginning with the Old Testament, tell of famines caused by locust hordes, and epidemics caused by mildew, blasting and rusts. When the pioneers moved into the great plains of Minnesota and the Dakotas, their crops were sometimes seriously damaged or destroyed as the result of grasshopper plagues, and their wheat and oats were often hard hit by rust epidemics. When the Mormons settled in Utah, their crops were seriously damaged by crickets—which to this day are known as Mormon crickets.

So we see that crop losses from pests and diseases were an old story long before the invention of pesticides. On numerous occasions in the distant past, natural biological control failed to hold pests in check, just as it cannot be relied upon alone today, to the exclusion of chemicals. Mother Nature has had a history of getting out of balance quite often, all down through history. An enormous number of species disappeared before man inhabited the earth. They apparently disappeared because they could not adapt rapidly enough to changes in the environment. So let's not be too hasty in blaming man for the disappearance of many of the defunct species. But if we are serious about preserving as many wildlife species as possible, then we should be more concerned about developing expanding wildlife research programs, constructive programs for improving wildlife habitats—and dissipate less of our resources in lawsuits, which after all primarily serve to fatten lawyers' incomes. Moreover, conservationists should be more concerned about slowing human population growth so that wildlife is not crowded out of existence.

It is my contention that we must have pesticides and use them properly to protect our crops and animals. I have unpleasant personal memories of the difficulties in growing crops before the advent of modern insecticides, weed killers and fungicides. I remember as a small boy walking behind my grandfather during the potato season. He would turn over the leaves of the potato plants to see if we could find adult Colorado potato beetles. When we found one, I would drown it in a small can of kerosene that I was carrying. But later there would always be egg clusters despite the tedious, laborious monitoring for adults. Again I would pick off the infested leaflets and submerge them in kerosene. Eventually, despite this vigilance, there were many young larvae, and so we would resort to toxic copper arsenate sprays.

On the weed control front, during school vacation I was given a hoe and turned loose in Canadian thistle patches in both the fields and pastures. I would chop thistles most of the summer, but when I returned to inspect the success of my hard work, I generally found two thistles for each one I had cut off.

Today there seems to be a sort of a nostalgia in certain sectors of our society and especially among the elite in the environmental movement. To them it looks so simple to observe the game from the sidelines, and decide what strategy should be used to control crop pests, without getting into the battle of sweat and frustration trying to increase food production. But I personally don't want to go back to the power end of the hoe, nor do I believe that anyone who has ever experienced such drudgery wants to return to those "good" old days.

Both in the United States and in developing countries there are many who dream of the day when pests can be successfully controlled by biological means. I dream such dreams also, but without much hope. It is my contention that we need to develop integrated approaches to pest control, employing improved cultural practices, biological control, and biological sexual trickery (such as the use of male steriles and pheremones), insect and disease resistant varieties, insofar as possible, and the wise use of the right types of chemical pesticides. But biological controls alone will often not be adequate to protect our crops and forests without supplementary proper use of pesticides. We should not soon forget the loss of 400,000 acres of Douglas fir timber in Oregon, Washington and Idaho in 1973, following two successive years of defoliation by the Tussock moth. The environmental groups and lawyers used legal tactics in 1972 to prevent the U. S. Forest Service and State Conservation Departments from spraying with DDT, which was known to be highly effective against this insect, using the argument that natural enemies, a bacterium and virus, would bring the insect infestation under control so that spraying was unnecessary. But nature decided differently. The moths, with the help of a very dry summer, destroyed the Douglas fir—yet the environmentalists and lawyers were still convinced they knew better how to manage our forests than did our professional foresters.

We have all read great horror stories about the improper use of pesticides. A strict interpretation of the Food and Drug Act of 1958 says that any chemical which produces a tumor (presumably carcinogenic) when applied to rats has to be banned; we have seen certain important chemicals banned under this act. One example of disastrous results of giving up pesticides is the rise of the incidence of malaria. Sri Lanka, formerly known as Ceylon, had reduced the number of cases of malaria to 17 in 1971. Their spray programs were then shelved, in part because they thought the problem was overcome, but primarily because of fear of being poisoned by DDT following the outcries against this chemical prior to its being banned in the United States. Now the number of malaria cases has increased from 17 to about 500,000. India has gone from about 125,000 in 1971 to about 3.5 million cases in 1975, and the figures are skyrocketing everywhere. We have two of our staff members ill with very serious cases of malaria at the present time. Both contracted the disease in a country where malaria was under control four years ago, but which today has severe epidemics because of abandoning the use of DDT. Currently spray programs with DDT and other chemicals are being reactivated in many countries. These are the results of actions taken to ban the use of chemicals without carefully weighing benefits against risks. We oversimplify. We want utopian environments with zero risks.

Using chemicals is like using medicine. If you are ill, you go to a doctor, and hopefully he diagnoses what is wrong with you. If it is a bacterial infection, let us say, he will probably give you an antibiotic or sulfa drug. If you use the medicine properly as directed, it may cure you. If you use it improperly, it might kill you.

The way some people talk about the balance of nature, they should examine their conscience before taking medicine to determine whether it is morally right to eliminate that poor little bacterium, or that nice long tapeworm or innocent looking roundworm that has invaded their bodies. If we really believe in control by the balance of nature, we should go the whole way. Then we should not vaccinate our children or grandchildren against any of the contagious diseases that have been conquered in the last 40 or 50 years. When they are sick, don't take them to the doctor. And we should convince our friends and neighbors to take similar action. Then we will soon see that there will be a new shift in this balance with nature. And it will indeed help solve the world population problem. Such widespread action probably would within two or three decades reduce world population to one-third or one-fourth of what it is today. This would solve our food production problems. But what chaos! Is that the kind of world we want to live in? I do not believe there are many people who really want to revert to placing human destiny in the hands of the balance of nature.

Increasing Agricultural Production in Developing Countries

What can be done then to increase food production in a developing country? One has to take a broad view and put the whole production package together, manipulating both the technological and economic factors. To begin, one must find out through research what nutrients have been depleted from the soil, and what fertilizers must be applied and at what dosages on different kinds of soil to correct these deficiencies. Then one has to breed a different kind of crop plant that will, insofar as possible, be resistant to the major diseases, more efficient in use of fertilizer and soil moisture, and that will produce more harvest per acre. Most cereal grains are produced for human consumption; the straw and stalks are by-products sometimes used for fuel or other purposes such as animal feeds, but the primary consideration is maximizing the production of grain per acre. Once the soil is fertilized, one has to be careful that one does not grow weeds rather than grain. When one starts fertilizing worn-out lands, the weeds which were also previously "starving to death" suddenly become aggressive. One must control them, either mechanically or by chemicals or by a combination of methods. And so too with insects—biologically, by employing sexual "trickery" when possible, or with the proper use of the right chemical at the right time.

Next, the technology developed through research has to be extended to the farmer. It has to be demonstrated on his farm or a neighbor's farm. When it is done in an experiment station, the small farmer is never convinced how much of the result is really due to the new technology and how much is due to witchcraft. The difference in yield between the old technology and the new has to be large enough that it is worth the risk for this subsistence farmer to change his methods. Unless the technology is really viable economically, he will not adapt. Then you have to marry the new technology to a realistic government economic agricultural policy which will assure the farmer that there will be a fair price at harvest. Otherwise as soon as the harvest starts, the grain price will plummet 50 percent or 60 percent and the grain merchant, who also very frequently happens to be the banker and moneylender, will buy the farmer's grain cheap; two months later the price will again be 150 percent higher than during the harvest.

The governments in these countries, if production is to be stimulated, must make sure that provisions are made to support agricultural prices, to buy grain at harvest, put it into warehouses, and feed it gradually into the market. The fertilizer has to be available on time, and also the credit to buy it. In order to achieve these conditions one must often convince heads of government that agriculture and food are important. I have tried to do this many times myself, sometimes in very unpleasant circumstances. A number of years ago, I felt obligated to say to one of the key ministers in a country with serious food problems: "Mr. Minister, with all due respect, unless this improved technology which is now available is put into application, and unless economic policies are adapted to stimulate food production, you won't be sitting in that chair two years from now, and your country will drift into economic and social chaos." Fortunately wise policies on fertilizer and grain pricing were adopted within two days' time, and within a few weeks the whole production picture was turned around. I have seen positive agricultural changes in many places in the past decade, but I have seen them disrupted again in the last two years, because of other factors, especially the energy crisis, I am sorry to say. It is a never-ending struggle.

I saw Indian wheat production, as a result of improved technology and stimulatory prices, rise from 400 million bushels in 1967 to a billion bushels in 1972. Then the country was caught in the petroleum crisis of 1973. India imports all of its petroleum and a third of its fertilizer, and it also was importing about a million tons of grain to supplement its own production at that time. It was approaching self-sufficiency, considering that much of the grain held in stock was given to Bangladesh refugees in the disastrous Pakistan war of 1972. But India was hit harder by the petroleum crisis than more privileged nations such as the United States. The same amounts of petroleum, grain, and fertilizer that India imported in 1971 at a cost of $530 million dollars, would in 1974 have cost $3.5 billion— and their total foreign exchange earnings were only about $2 billion. So you can see that the economy of the country was very vulnerable. The OPEC nations, of course, have profited enormously by the change in petroleum prices, but I call your attention to the plight of at least 20 Third World nations that have food and fertilizer deficits and also are petroleum importers. It is they who have suffered more than the industrialized developed nations. It often appears to me that most Americans believe the recent petroleum shortages and the very modest increase in domestic gasoline prices they pay is a political hoax fostered jointly by the OPEC nations and American oil companies. They still fail to believe that there is an imminent petroleum crisis ahead. I wish it were so simple!

The Carrying Capacity of the Earth

What is the carrying capacity of the earth from the standpoint of food? Before I attempt to answer, I have to ask: At what standard of living? What are you willing to settle for? Is it the standard of living of America, or of India, or of the People's Republic of China? I recently spent a month in China.

I was tremendously impressed by what I saw there. The agricultural production of that country has gone up enormously since the revolution in 1949, and especially since 1960. All this has become possible because the highest order of importance in development was given to agriculture. Eighty percent of the people are on the land and they work hard. The crops that we saw were excellent. They were summer crops, especially rice, corn, sorghum and cotton.

Until 1960 there was no chemical fertilizer used in China. But they had maintained for decades a much higher level of soil fertility and crop yields than India, a country of similar population density under relatively similar climatic conditions. What was the difference? Partly it is the way animal waste, human waste, and plant wastes are used in China; this has been a long-time part of their culture. It is also interesting to know that they produce 260 millions hogs, which is roughly 5 times the number produced in the United States in most years. But I'm not at all sure which is the primary product and which is the secondary; I have the feeling that pig manure is first and pork chops second in order of importance, because of the role of organic compost and fertilizer in the past agriculture of the Chinese people.

But the government recognized as early as 1960 that organic fertilizer would no longer be sufficient to produce the food needed for their enormous and rapidly growing population. And so they began to install small chemical nitrogen fertilizing plants based on using lignite coal to produce anhydrous ammonia, and converting it to ammonium bicarbonate, a 17 percent solid nitrogenous fertilizer. There were 800 of those plants in operation in 1974. They are small and dispersed throughout the country, perhaps to circumvent problems of transport. But despite the domestic production of chemical nitrogen, by 1973 the Chinese also had become the world's largest importer of urea and other solid nitrogenous fertilizer, mostly from Japan.

When the OPEC petroleum embargo went on in October 1973, Japan cut back its production of fertilizer by about 50 percent, and within six weeks China made a decision to install ten 1,000-ton-a-day anhydrous ammonia plants and urea converters, which represented about one and a half billion dollars in capital investment in the plants alone. And they contracted for the best nitrogen fertilizer engineering technology available in the world, with Kellogg Engineering of Houston, Texas. Since then, they have added three more plants to their production plans; these are being built by Tokyo Engineering Co. China is changing its whole infrastructure to supply raw materials for these plants and to distribute the products. This involves opening new gas fields, building gas pipelines, warehouses, and transport systems. The total investment that will be going into this program before it is completed may represent a cost of seven to eight billion dollars.

How do the people live? I never saw a hungry person in China; they all looked well fed and adequately clothed. I never saw people work more diligently for long hours. Fields were tidy and neat with no weeds. I asked a distinguished senior Chinese scientist, who happened to be assigned to guide our team of 10 visiting American scientists, sponsored under an exchange program by the National Academy of Sciences: "How do you get the people to work like this? There must be lazy people here as there are everywhere in the world." He replied: "It's very easy. Those who don't work, don't eat." I said, "Supposing there's a lazy son or daughter who is not ill but refuses to work." "Well," he said, "this might go on for a few days or weeks, but there would be peer-group pressure, and sooner or later the neighbors would be pointing their fingers also at the parents, saying that they are not good citizens and had better straighten out their family. When it is done by quite a few neighbors, they get the idea."

I don't want to leave the impression that life in China is

beautiful. But the masses have the basic necessities. However, about all one can aspire to at the present time is adequate food and clothing. Bicycles and wristwatches are considered luxury items. Yet it is undoubtedly a much better life for the masses than what they had before the revolution. But no one knows how many millions were sacrificed to establish the system, and no one knows how many thousands were lost while involved in rekindling the fires of revolution, in the cultural revolution of the mid-sixties. We have heard about what was done to play down the old Confucianism. This was done partly and perhaps largely to orient science toward the application of knowledge to serve the needs of the people. The Red Guard was stirred up and turned loose in the universities, which created all sorts of havoc and a good excuse to close the universities and to send the professors of agricultural sciences to the communes, the engineers and chemists to the factories, the doctors from very large city hospitals to rural communes. In the communes they were, as the cliché goes, "reeducated" by the lower and middle class peasants so that they could apply science and make it work for the people. Chairman Mao was apparently unwilling during his lifetime to see stifling bureaucracy destroy the nation's agricultural potential as happened in the Soviet Union, and his answer was to rekindle the fires of the revolution via the Cultural Revolution and the destruction of Confucianism.

But top priority and progress in agriculture has not been limited to any one system of government in Asia. Look at what has happened with technical improvements in agriculture in South Korea and in Taiwan. There has been tremendous progress in both countries in increasing yields through application of improved science and technology. So it can be done under various systems of government, but it requires a certain discipline. I dread to think what would happen to our privileged American society if we were required to work as hard and be subjected to some of the disciplines that have been imposed under other governments. What part of our society would need to be destroyed before it could be reeducated and subjected to a different political system which would also involve loss of much personal freedom? This is certainly not pleasant to think about. These are questions to ponder as we look around about us in the world today.

Lifeboat Ethics of Survival

Today there are some people who advocate triage or lifeboat ethics for national survival. They advocate letting the food-deficit nations with huge fast-growing populations starve. This implies that as a nation we could isolate ourselves from the world around about us. But look at the position of the United States today. We are not self-sufficient in virtually all non-renewable resources as we were 50 years ago. We import 80-100 percent of 12 minerals that are basic to metallurgical industries. Then there is another group of about 14 minerals and basic resources of which we import from 40 to 80 percent; in that category are petroleum, iron, copper, zinc, and lead. What would be do without these imports? How would we keep our factories running? What would the unemployment be and the social unrest if we tried to get along without them? We are now part of the total world community, whether we like it or not. It is not 1930; it is 1976 and the world has shrunk.

The food situation in densely populated countries is very serious but it is not hopeless. If agriculture is given its merited support and allocation of funds, it will be possible to expand food production faster than population growth for the next two decades at least. Food reserves must be reestablished to protect against unfavorable crop years.

In the case of cereal crop production, wheat in many areas of Asia and Africa has made more progress in the last decade than any other cereal. Production more than doubled in both

India and Pakistan during the seven-year period from 1965 to 1972. Wheat production can be doubled again within a decade if adequate quantities of fertilizer are made available, if diseases are kept under control by aggressive plant breeding programs, and if wise economic policies are followed. The scientific information and technology is now available that would enable these countries also to double their maize and sorghum production within the next 10 years. New varieties of rice with appropriate technology for its cultivation promise a breakthrough in rice production in India, and hopefully in Bangladesh, within a few years.

These changes will, of course, only be holding actions; agricultural production cannot increase indefinitely, and neither can population. Aggressive food production programs and policies would allow time for effective population policies to be introduced and begin to take effect. I have seen the myth of the non-receptivity of the peasant farmer to changes in farming practices vanish whenever effective new technology and stimulatory economic policy have been brought together in proper relationship. This leads me to believe that the illiterate peasant in densely populated countries will also respond positively to reducing his family size if a physiologically safe, foolproof, simple, humane birth control method is developed and made known to him through an educational plan which encourages its widespread adoption.

It appears to me that it is better for all of us, each in his own way, to try to educate the world masses about the seriousness of the "population monster," and thereby slow population growth, than recklessly and unwittingly to provoke the wrath of extremist guerrillas in developing nations by advocating lifeboat or triage survival by withholding food. With the destructive powers that are present in the world—and which could well fall into the hands of extremist terrorists—we must recognize that in their frenzy and wrath they might trigger off a series of events that could pollute the atmosphere and bring about a solution to the world human population problem for thousands of years, or even solve it permanently, by the annihilation of *Homo sapiens.*

Rather, it seems to me, the United States should recognize the enormous value of its current agricultural food, fiber and forest production and its even greater future production potential. In recent years we have exported more than $20 billion dollars of these products annually. We should recognize that food, fiber and forest products are renewable resources that can be exported or traded for non-renewable resources that we must import in ever-increasing quantities. It behooves the American people to foster wise policies that promote education, research, and investment in agriculture, rather than see it strangled by unwise bureaucratic regulations that are being advocated by some poorly informed extremists in the environmental movement.

There are those who believe we are on the verge of being poisoned out of existence. They visualize carcinogens in the air, water and every bite of food we eat. Despite such criticism, we live a longer and more pleasant life than our parents or grandparents. Since most infectious diseases that formerly took the life of many in childhood, youth and middle age have been brought under control within the last 40 years, more people die at a later age from other diseases, such as cancer and heart troubles. Many that a generation ago would have died at an early age, because of genetic susceptibility to one or another infectious disease, survive to die at a later date from the still bewildering and poorly understood group of cancer diseases, giving the laymen the feeling that there is a startling increase in incidence of cancer. The present hysteria about cancer in the environment and food stems largely from the fact we seem to forget the self-evident truth that all that is born must suffer and die. It also raises the question of whether it is wise to perpetuate life beyond the time when life remains enjoyable. Each generation continues to look for the fountain of perpetual youth just as did Ponce de Leon and many before him. And we will never find it, but imagine the world disaster that would result on the human population front were it attainable.

Let me close with a comment about the claim that we would currently have no world food problem if Americans, Canadians, and Europeans would eat less meat. It is true that we would be able to feed a great many more people if our diet was based primarily on grains and pulses or grain legumes of various kinds, in the right proportions from the standpoint of amino acids as well as calorie intake. In India a ton of grain will feed between five and six people for a year. In the United States and Canada it will feed only a little more than one person because so much of the grain is converted to meat, eggs, and milk. But changing food customs is not simple. I served on the committee of 21 so-called eminent scientists that was to make recommendations to the Secretary-General of the Rome World Food Conference. I wasn't convinced we were very eminent by the time we had spent three days and most of three nights disagreeing with each other. Time and again someone would say: "Now, if we just gave up eating one hamburger a week, we wouldn't have this crisis." I kept saying, "Would you please tell me how this hamburger is going to convert itself back into grain and then fly across the ocean in time to feed the hungry people in Bangladesh?"

What would we do with the enormous quantities of corn which the United States produces—5.7 billion bushels this year —if we did not feed most of it to livestock? We do export several hundred million bushels that are used directly as human food—primarily in Mexico, Central and South America, and in four or five countries in Central Africa where corn is eaten as a preferred basic food. But with those exceptions, corn is not eaten in large quantities as a basic food. The remainder, more than 5 billion bushels, is fed to livestock in the United States, or exported to Europe or Japan where it is fed to animals. The cereal shortage in the last two years has been mainly in wheat and rice. Now you cannot change food habits overnight; it can be done only slowly and gradually, over several decades. I am sure we need to look ahead; it means we have to teach people in many foreign countries how to use corn directly as food. But it cannot be done in a few weeks in times of crisis.

Suppose that we tried to grow other crops instead of corn. What would happen to farm income in the corn belt? It would plummet and we would destroy our farmers and our food production capacity. Couldn't we plant wheat, which is widely used as human food? I was recently looking at the farm records in Iowa for the 1880s; wheat was grown much more widely than corn at that time, and, surprisingly, it yielded more per acre than corn. This brings out the tremendous progress that has been achieved by agricultural scientists and farmers in adapting corn, and more recently soybeans, to the eco-system of the United States corn belt. Certainly if we tried to put wheat back into this area precipitously we would have all sorts of disease epidemics. Grain yields would be much lower than corn. In 15 or 20 years we could do something about increasing the disease resistance, but we could not do it overnight. We almost certainly would never achieve the grain yields with wheat that are obtained with corn, for the latter crop is ideally adapted to the ecology of the corn belt. We would have no success whatsoever if we tried to introduce Indian or Asiatic rice, the other cereal that has been in short supply in recent years; the climate and the soils here are just not right. Nor do I believe that even our most elite new ecologist would recommend that we try to introduce northern wild rice as a substitute crop for corn in the corn belt.

In the long run, then, we should encourage and teach the use of corn as human food in food-deficit countries, and we can work on developing other high-yielding crops to grow here at home. But in the short run the abandonment of meat would be disastrous to the farm economy and would destroy the food production potential of this important agricultural region. Our goal in the long run must be to increase the production of food in all countries to feed a hungry world—while we work aggressively at taming the population monster. Time is running out on us. Since I started talking, there are 11,000 more people to be fed.

6

Food and Development

At the outset let me say that I believe in problem solving, which may simply mean that I am optimistic. I do not believe that there are problems of consequence in the world that cannot be solved. I also think that the past history of the world indicates that people really do have the capacity to adjust to change. And I believe there is a reasonable chance that we *can* change in time to avert catastrophe.

The world has many problems. The problem of peace obviously is one that remains unsolved. The problem of our environment—our world environment—also remains unsolved. The problem of population is crucial, and the problem of poverty— the fact that something like one fourth of all the people in the world live on less than $75 a year, and perhaps half of the people in the world on less than $200. Those are unsolved problems that have to be solved if we are going to survive. But I believe that in fact we have the capacity—the human capacity. The question is really whether we have the will to exert that capacity to bring about the changes necessary to avoid a catastrophic end.

It is not a question of deciding which portion of the human

race to save—that would be a political decision which I do not think could be made—but rather the challenge of making those institutional and technological changes that are required if the world's needs are to be met, both in agricultural development and in population control.

I think we made a beginning at the World Food Conference in Rome in 1974—a bare beginning. That conference was in many ways unsuccessful, but I think it was an important beginning. And I think the Seventh Special Session of the United Nations General Assembly in 1975 marked another important step, also a bare beginning, toward cooperation. It is incumbent on all of us to see that these beginnings are followed by a continuing application of man's most creative and imaginative efforts in the years ahead. Although we did not accomplish many of the things that most of us had hoped for, either at the Rome conference or the Special Session, I think these conferences were most useful. The Rome conference, for example, centered world attention on the problems of hunger—both the short-term problem of immediate famine, and the harder problem, the long-term challenge of increasing world production. And the United Nations not long before that had held the conference on population at Bucharest, which centered world attention on the problem of population growth. Because of that conference in Rome, people all over the world, and Americans in particular, came to realize that the world faces a major famine problem.

Since the Rome conference, however, there has been a growing feeling that the world's food problems have disappeared, or at least receded, perhaps because the famine of 1974 was relieved by emergency food aid from our country and from other countries. We pitched together, we worked very hard, we got the food aid together, and we avoided a famine which otherwise would have been enormous in its dimensions. But the problems and the dangers are still very real. Some countries, in fact, may face greater dangers from starvation today than they did at that time. Some 40,000 people are reported to have died of starvation, for example, in the horn of Africa, in Somalia and Ethiopia, and thousands more will die if the drought continues in those countries.

Four hundred million people a year around the world—that's twice the population of the United States, or almost one eighth of the world's population—suffer from malnutrition. That does not mean that they will die of starvation; it means that they are so seriously suffering from malnutrition that they will be permanently damaged mentally or physically. One out of every eight people in the world—that is the dimension of the problem of malnutrition. And during this last year, the world's food reserves have fallen, and the world's population has grown by 75 million people. So the problem is clear and its dimensions are understandable. This year's global harvests are expected to be about 3 percent above last year's, although there have been weather problems in several of the producing areas. The Russian grain crop has shown the biggest shortfall, as we are all very much aware. But Western Europe and India are other areas that have had to cut back on their estimates of grain for this year. And world reserves are at an all-time low; most estimates are that we now have only twenty-seven days' supply of food on hand. Bad weather that would have had little impact in past years can now cause serious food shortages.

Through much of our recent history we have had enormous surpluses. There was a time not very long ago when all across the Midwest we had bins full of corn and, farther west, of wheat. We were spending $1 million a day just to store grain, and we were spending significantly more than that not to produce on a lot of the land, because we didn't know what to do with it. So the shortage is a recent thing that has occurred not simply because of population growth, but also because of the unusual weather conditions that we have seen since 1972. Most experts agree that it will be impossible to meet the growing demand for food in future years without dramatic improvements in agricultural productivity in the developing countries.

We are not at the edge of disaster yet if we get anything approaching average weather. We know the productive capacity that this country alone has, and we know the productive capacity of other countries. But nevertheless, sooner or later the statistics add up to disaster if we do not make the technological and psychological changes that are necessary. In short, the urgent problems at the Rome conference are still as urgent as they were before the conference. The United States dominated the world grain supply (not the world grain production, but the amount that is put on the market). Half of all the grain that is put on the international market comes from the United States. People talk about the control that the Arabs have on oil; they actually control only 48 percent of the world's oil (OPEC controls more, but the Arab states, only 48 percent). So we have a greater hold on a much more basic commodity, food. What I am saying is that those of us here, especially in the United States, but also in the developed world, have a special responsibility. There is now at last an official recognition of the fact that the old game of losers and winners will not work any more in what is accurately called an interdependent world. And we must find a way to work together in this world.

Let me review briefly where we were prior to the Rome food conference. In the 1960s and early 1970s the world saw unprecedented rates of economic growth, ranging between 5 and 6 percent per year. And this growth had consequences that few people, let alone the economists, anticipated. It led not only to shortages of many commodities, but to serious ecological overload, problems of inflation, and a range of political and social problems. The annual increase in effective demand for food is a good example of that. In the early 1900s the annual increase in world food demand was in the range of 4 million tons. By

1950, it had increased to 12 million tons. By the early 1970s it was running in the range of 25 to 30 million tons. The global demand for food, that is, the total consumption of food in the world, is expected to increase from 1.2 billion tons in 1971, to 1.7 billion tons in 1985. Of that total tonnage, the 1 billion people in the affluent parts of the world consume half, and the other 3 billion get the other half. So we eat three times as well, roughly speaking.

Meanwhile the developed countries were putting virtually the last available land under production, and turning ever more heavily to the use of fertilizer and improved seed strains to increase production. We have some potential left, certainly, but we don't have much land sitting around unused. We have used up the easy potential; it gets tougher and much more expensive as we go along. The same trend was occurring in some of the developing countries as well; the result was an increasing dependence on chemical fertilizer in all parts of the world. More than 80 million tons of fertilizer were used worldwide in 1974—four-fifths of it here in the developed world, although the developing world with the Green Revolution was beginning to use it. And as far as the developed countries were concerned, we were using so much fertilizer that we were reaching the point of diminishing returns. And then came the events of 1973 and 1974. Serious droughts had drastically limited food supplies rather suddenly. We used up our surpluses, and the Middle East conflict leading to the oil embargo and the sharply increased energy crisis put a whole new view on the problem of fertilizer.

The initial responses of the world's decision-makers were anything but global in nature; they rarely are in times of stress and strain. The newly organized OPEC countries, feeling their oats, began a five-fold increase in the price of oil. The affluent countries, through the Organization for Economic Cooperation and Development (OECD), set themselves up as a kind of counter-force to the OPEC countries, and an economic war began. Among the unfortunate developments of this period was a decision by the United States to cut back on overseas shipments of fertilizer, thereby reducing the chances for adequate food production in other areas of the world—particularly in those countries that needed it most, the developing countries, where the Green Revolution program had just begun to get under way, and of course it was dependent upon fertilizer.

In addition, the United States drastically reduced its food aid programs in order to make food sales to other affluent nations. By early 1974 this country was not implementing even the semblance of a global food policy beyond that of seeking the maximum dollar gain from agricultural exports, which rose from $9 billion in 1972 to $22 billion in 1974. By 1974 our food aid had dropped to less than 40 percent of the average volume in the late '60s and early '70s. To cite two figures: in 1966 the food assistance that we gave to the developing world was 18 million tons; in 1975 it was 5 million tons. Increasingly, also, our limited food aid has gone for political purposes, not to help hungry people. We know, for example, that in 1974 over half of all the food aid we gave went to Indochina, where much of it was sold under the Title I program on the open market, and simply converted to the war effort. And we have greatly lowered the total volume of food aid. I am always surprised to hear Secretary Butz in Rome and other places talking about how the United States has in the past been the great leader in food aid. He is absolutely right— it is a thing of the past, because it has gone down and down and down. Certainly we *were* the great leaders in that area, but let us not take credit any more for the kind of aid we once gave.

Now the approach to food issues at the World Food Conference was one of treating food problems as global in scale. That was one of the great advantages, it seems to me, of getting 130 countries in one building to focus on the fact that this is a global problem, not a national problem or a hemispheric problem. In my judgment it is not even a problem of the developed world and the developing world. It is a problem for the whole world and warrants an unprecedented global response, as do almost all of our economic problems. Global goals and objectives were set, and means were proposed for meeting them over the long and medium and short run.

The short-term problem is a shortage of food. If you are starving to death there is only one thing that we can do if we want to save your life, and that is to give you food, or the money to buy food. We cannot lecture you on whether or not your grandparents or your parents should have practiced population control, if we want to keep you alive. We cannot debate the issue of agricultural development, if we want to keep you alive; we have to give you food. That is the short-term problem of famine, but to give you food solves no long-term problem. Food aid does keep people from suffering brain damage or other physical damage from malnutrition. But the next day you have the same problem, and the day after that, and the day after that, so the long-term effect of famine, the long-term problem of malnutrition, has to be solved by helping countries to develop their ability to feed themselves. I think it was Gandhi who said that if you give a person a fish, he eats for a day; if you teach him how to fish, he eats for the rest of his life. Food aid is a band-aid; it keeps people alive. Development assistance, helping people to develop the ability to feed themselves, is the long-term solution.

And, of course, there is a third element to which we have to address ourselves before we are finished, and that is the problem of this enormous increase in population. So we face the short-term problem of feeding people, the long-term problem of adequate production through fertilizer and technology— all the things that develop agricultural production—and then simultaneously, and an essential element of our total problem, a way of checking population. This is the agenda before us.

Now, with regard to fertilizer production and food production, I think it is clear that the potential for the world is enormous. In the developing world the potential is so enormous that we should not throw up our hands and say, "There is no way that we can feed those people on the earth today or in the next decade or in the next century." We know that both fertilizer and food production can be increased substantially. For one thing—and I cite only one of hundreds that I might cite—the gas that is being flared in the Middle East is a resource that can and should be used for fertilizer production. We know that there are still millions of acres that lie fallow in the Sudan, and many other African countries that not long ago I visited, that simply need a plow. We know that there are millions of acres in the world that need nothing but water to make them fertile—some of it costly, but some of it not so costly. So let us not assume that this limited world now has no more potential for growth in food production.

I think the various proposals at the Rome Conference for establishing a whole family of institutions to address every major aspect of the world food problem are an important beginning. Already, for example, the United Nations General Assembly has established the World Food Council. And already the important consultative group on food production and investment has come into existence to help insure action on key investment and production problems in the developing world. While we were very disappointed at the time that no firm decision was made to increase food aid to meet the immediate famine problem, nevertheless, President Ford eventually did decide to increase American aid in fiscal 1975 by an additional 2 million tons. And equally important, when we came back from that conference we passed a resolution both on the Senate floor and in the House which said that 70 percent of all the food aid we sent had to go to hungry countries —to those nations listed by the United Nations as most severely affected. We were not going to take those diminishing volumes of food and simply send them to Vietnam or Chile or South Korea or some place where we had a political problem that we wanted to address ourselves to.

Also recommended by the conference was an international fund for agricultural development. If we are going to solve the long-term problem, we have to begin in the affluent world to set aside a small part of our affluence to help with the problem of agricultural development. Agreement was also reached at the conference for a comprehensive approach to increasing fertilizer production, particularly in the energy-exporting countries. A system of world food security to involve the major grain exporters and importers, and an improved policy for food aid—all of these things came out of the Rome conference and are now emplaced or at least in the stage of implementation.

I think Rome was an important turning point. I know very well that none of these goals have been fulfilled, and it is going to be up to us—those of us in this country, particularly, and in the rest of the industrialized and developed world—to see that in fact they are carried out. Whether the additional funds will be forthcoming, to increase external assistance for raising agricultural and fertilizer production, is going to be up to us. I think that this country ought to raise its assistance from the $1.5 billion of the past to something in the range of $5 billion, when you remember that we have a budget of some $360 billion. Without substantial additional funds for fertilizer and for agricultural development, the developing countries are not going to be able to increase their agricultural production adequately. It's as simple as that. We know that the potential is there, if we are prepared to help.

The question is not whether we have the capacity, the ability, or the affluence to undertake food aid, development assistance and population control, but rather whether we have the will. The argument that we in the developed part of the world simply do not have the resources or the money to help those in the developing world just cannot be scientifically supported. Food aid, for example, this last year, was $1.5 billion. Development aid was about $1.5 billion—stretched to its greatest it could be conceived to be that high. So we're talking about a current food aid and development program of some $3 billion at most. Can we afford more? Could we afford to double or triple that? I think we could, and I think it would be a good investment. If we can afford $100 billion for the defense budget, we can afford to help countries develop the ability to feed themselves. Let me just cite one weapons system. I hate to pick on this one because I've heard it picked on before, but let us take the Trident, since it is such a striking example. We are about to build ten new Tridents; the Secretary of Defense says we ought to build 11. Each Trident costs $1.63 billion, according to the new figures. They used to talk about $1.5 billion for one Trident, which happens to be exactly what we spent on food aid last year. And we are embarking on ten, to say nothing of the B-1 and many other things. What does a Trident submarine get you? What do we get for that? It has only one mission in the Navy—only one—as a launching pad for 16 additional nuclear missiles, each one of which will contain ten MIRV warheads, or 160 warheads in all, which, as with our present Polaris and Poseidon, will be aimed at a city or a target in the Soviet Union. That is what we are going to get for our $1.63 billion.

Now one might argue that we need more nuclear missiles aimed at the Soviet Union in this period of detente. But if you remember that we currently have in our arsenal 30,000 nuclear warheads of one kind or another, you begin to wonder whether that $1.5 billion is the best way that we, in an interdependent world, can spend our affluence. And it seems to me that if we are really interested in human problems, we must begin to face up to them. I am not talking about unilateral disarmament—I wish I could be optimistic enough to favor that—but I am talking about holding down the rate of increase in the arms race. The Soviet Union and we both know that there is no way either of us could shoot a nuclear weapon at the other without totally destroying both of us. We are both fully aware of that, and yet we continue to build nuclear weapons. And we do not have the wherewithal to face up to these other problems of the world. And if the United States and the Soviets—we are the two who spend the money, almost in equal amounts—if we are not able to get some kind of handle on that arms race, we are going to use up much of the world's resources for no great purpose, while telling all the developing world that we cannot possibly afford to help them.

I want to talk briefly about the population question, because I think it is so closely related. That problem is perhaps the greatest—greater than the question of food aid, since, at least in the next few decades we can provide the food aid. Obviously we have the ability and the affluence to provide development assistance. The question is how to check population growth. I am not a population authority, but my own feeling is that you do not check population growth simply by the distribution of information and contraceptive devices, much as I favor that. I favor spending as much as is reasonable to do that; I think it's an excellent idea and I'm 100 percent for it. But the fact of the matter is that people do not stop having children until they have a will to stop having children and to use contraceptive devices, even if they are educated and have them available.

We know historically that the countries who control their population are the countries with economic stability. And you do not get economic stability by letting people starve. You get economic stability first and foremost through agricultural development, by helping the smallest farms, the poorest of the poor, through the most basic kind of transfer of technology and information, to raise the food to eat. These countries, after all, are labor intensive; they are not capital intensive. They have the ability and the potential to develop food. Why do they have so many children? Because the average farm in most of the developing world is something under twelve acres. If you have no technology of any kind and no capital, you have to have labor. And that means children. You do not farm ten or twelve acres with two or three children. Moreover, in these economic systems you have no social security system, no food stamp program, national government help. You are dependent upon yourself and your children, and if you want eight children to live, you had better have sixteen or twenty. If you want four to live, you had better have six or eight or ten, whatever the statistics show. So there is every economic motivation to have children if you hope to live to an old age and have somebody feed you. And one cannot simply say to these people that because the world's population is growing they have to stop having children, and should use these contraceptive devices. That does not work. They are not worried about the world's population; they do not even know about it.

Now I do not happen to subscribe to the idea that the answer to the population problem is to let people starve. First of all I do not think it would work. If I understand the historical trends in population, it is precisely in those countries where you have the highest death rate that you have the highest birthrate. To let people starve does not cause your population to decline; in the long run, it causes birthrates to increase, believe it or not. Look at the countries of the world. Where do we have the greatest death rate from starvation and malnutrition? In Bangladesh. Where do we have the greatest birthrate and the greatest increase in population in absolute figures? In Bangladesh. And wherever you have affluent countries, almost without exception, you have a lower growth rate. So I do not support the idea that if you start letting half the world starve to death they are suddenly going to decline in birthrates. I think they will increase even faster, because that is what history has shown us. If you want to have four children, you do not start with eight any more if the death rate goes up, but with sixteen. How else are you going to live and farm those twelve acres? We would have much more starvation, and much more malnutrition and retardation—a world of half-people, but they are going to be there, they are not all going to die. They are going to continue to multiply. And the only way you can change that is through economic stability, in my judgment.

Finally, I just cannot accept the idea that somehow we can let a certain part of the world die. Who would make that decision on behalf of our government? The President? Which countries are going to be written off? Is that going to be the decision for Henry Kissinger, or Secretary Butz, or is the Congress going to vote on it? It seems to me that Lifeboat Ethics is an interesting theory to deal with. I think anything of that kind ought to be discussed, but if one tried to put it into practice and have a vote, or have some dictator decide, we would begin to see the difficulties of implementing that view.

Furthermore it seems to me that we would reject it if we really accept the idea of interdependence, if we really believe that we are dependent upon the developing world for many of our basic resources. We now have in the United Nations 105 nations of the world in the so-called non-aligned group with real leadership. They are not going to simply lie back and starve, I can assure you. In that group of non-aligned are the OPEC countries, and many other countries with the most basic raw materials that the industrialized world needs. I think a much better approach is to understand our dependency, our interdependency, to believe that we are in this world together. I am not here to preach morality, but I must say I do not see how we could live in a world in which we said that one person, one human being, has a life that is of more value than another human being. I think we must send food aid as well as assistance in agricultural and economic development.

7

Kenneth Boulding
Peggy Barlett
Senator Dick Clark

Panel
on Food and Development

KENNETH BOULDING: I have no criticisms of Senator Clark. The only thing I can do is to add one or two points. One point which I think we have neglected is the crucial significance of the status of women in all these problems. Part of the difficulty in technology transfer is that most of the food of the world is produced by women—and all of the people who give advice are men. They don't see the women; women are the most invisible objects in the world. Even anthropologists often don't seem to understand that there are women; they never notice half of the human race. Particularly in the tropical countries women are just crucial in agriculture, and yet nobody pays any attention to them. Very often the introduction of even simple technology has the impact of destroying the previous status of women. You get the men behind their little tractors, or whatever, and then the women are worse off than they were before. This is something that nobody pays enough attention to. And of course it is a well-known fact that women have babies and therefore have something to do with population; when it comes to population control, on the whole it's the women who have to say "no", isn't it?

A second comment is that the importance of protein is often overlooked. We just think of food in general, but one of the major world problems is protein deficiency. This is a question of the quality of food rather than of the quantity. The fact is that today we are raising hundreds of millions of defective human beings simply because protein deficiency has such an appalling impact on the development of children, and particularly on their mental capacity. This is no way to run a space ship. One of the interesting possibilities is to think of yeast as the major domestic animal instead of chickens or pigs. With yeast you can eat the whole thing and you can even drink its excrement. And our agricultural people haven't put anywhere near enough attention into this. If you take the cassava, which is the great food reserve of the tropics, there is no protein in it at all. I am assured by my biological colleagues (especially Professor David Rogers of the University of Colorado) that if you throw it into a dirty old pond and let it ferment and let the yeast get at it, you obtain 10 percent protein out of it. One of our problems is that science is a narrow-minded, temperate zone subculture; it doesn't know anything about the tropics. If we train these people in Minnesota and then they go back to the tropics, we've created an enormous amount of that import called trained incapacity. The kind of thing you can get away with in Minnesota you can't get away with in the tropics.

PEGGY BARLETT: I am in agreement with the kinds of points that Senator Clark made, and Kenneth Boulding has stolen some of my thunder about women. I am intrigued by the fact that the same three elements keep coming up: 1) increasing food production, 2) distributing the food, and 3) controlling world population. Clearly, the latter point is the limiting factor, and we will have to deal with it sooner or later, depending on whether we can increase food production.

I was unhappy with the generalizations which Dr. Hardin

made about the causes of population growth, particularly the idea that food aid is a major cause. I was very pleased when the Senator discussed what motivates people to have children. I agree that we need to look at the decision-making process of the peasant family and the fact that you need children to run a peasant economic system. If there are no kinds of social security, asking peasants to cut back on the number of children that they have is in some cases asking them to commit suicide. We need to look at the cost of producing a child for a family versus the amount that that child produces for the family. That balance makes a family decide how many children they will have. The cost of producing an unskilled laborer in India is amazingly low—considering that by the time that child is five years old it is already producing more than it is consuming. We also need to consider the cost of not producing the child; how many peasant families simply cannot afford the cost of not having many children? One Ecuadorian Indian that I know was married to a woman who had had 13 children, and only one of them had lived. This man was very poor; he had only one son to support him.

When we look anthropologically at the causes of population growth and the recent decline in growth in the last 25 years, we find three factors surfacing over and over again: standard of living, amount of education, and employment opportunities for women outside the home. I'm very much in favor of population programs being tied to food aid, as long as we are aware that these three factors are what cause population to decline. Are we doing something with our food aid which is increasing the standard of living? Are we increasing education? Are we providing alternative employment opportunities for women outside the home?

Providing contraception, as the Senator pointed out, is not sufficient. I'm afraid I don't completely share his optimism about contraception. I don't believe we have yet a safe, effective, cheap contraceptive method available, and I think Kenneth Boulding's point about men making decisions is one reason for this. Medical scientists have been saying for years that it is much easier to produce a contraceptive for men than a contraceptive for women, but men have been doing the research and producing contraceptives for women. Until we have a safe, cheap method, I think we should be a little more humble than we are about our population planning programs. I am not opposed to these programs, and I believe that we must allow all women to have a choice, but let us be aware that our technology has great limits.

Returning to the three themes which I noted, let us look at the remaining two from the viewpoint of the Indian peasant. With respect to increasing food production, the Green Revolution is the showcase. To what extent has the Green Revolution aided the standard of living of the people in the rural areas of India? According to many researchers, the Green Revolution has made no dent in rural poverty. The Green Revolution is a package of agricultural changes which are used primarily by the most wealthy farmers, the largest land owners. The increased income accruing from these new methods has not benefited the poor. So if we increase the amount of production, are we benefiting those who are starving? More than 50 percent of the rural people of India are living at the barest minimum, as defined by the Indian government—15 Rupees per month. We can attempt to double the production of wheat and rice, but these commodities are sold, and that lowest 50 percent has no more money than they did before to buy them. In fact, as a result of the Green Revolution, as much as 80 percent of the rural population in some provinces has experienced a relative decline in standard of living. The gap between the rich and poor is now much greater than it ever was.

The same kinds of problems arise concerning food aid. If we in the food producing nations are exporting food, there is often an assumption that the poorest people are getting it. Some of our food aid is distributed directly to famine areas and is given away free, but the majority of it is sold. And, again, who can afford to buy the wheat and rice that we are sending abroad? If we are just dealing with the question of food aid we are not dealing with this question of poverty at all. Whether we are talking about population control or food aid, we keep coming back to the same problems: standard of living, health, education, employment opportunities, and so forth. Therefore, economic development, which Garrett Hardin suggested is the cause of population growth, I see also as the cure.

What would be the cost of the kinds of things I'm suggesting? The Senator advises me that in 1975 we spent $11 billion on military aid and police training in Third World countries. Suppose that we wanted to eradicate illiteracy, since we know that education leads to lowering population growth. How much would it cost to eradicate illiteracy in the world? According to UNESCO it would cost $1.6 billion for five years—a seventh of what we are spending for military aid and police training. We know that a family planning program will not work unless accompanied by medical care. How much would it cost? According to Lester Brown, full maternal health, child health, and family planning programs for the world would cost $2 billion a year. So I would conclude in strong agreement with the Senator that we have the means and we lack only the will.

DICK CLARK: I think that Professor Boulding's point on the status of women in a developing world is a very relevant one. In regard to agricultural research, there is a section of the foreign aid bill which authorizes funds for U.S. agricultural colleges, the University of Minnesota and Iowa State among others, to assist in the transfer of technology and information to the developing world. I think in theory it makes a lot of sense;

we certainly know some things that could be transferred. But I think basically it's not the right approach. The great danger, which Professor Boulding referred to, is to assume that somehow this kind of transfer to the tropics or to other places can take place with ease. But we can't just transfer Iowa or Minnesota farms to Africa or to Southern Asia. The average Iowa farm now has something over $200,000 invested in it. We have enormous tractors and combines; almost nothing that I know of on an Iowa farm is transferable to the farms I visited in South Africa or Asia; even the seed has to be different. We should help the poorest farmers overseas, about whom Professor Barlett spoke so eloquently, and the smallest farms where the productive capacity is. There can be a transfer of technology and a transfer of information, perhaps, but of the most basic kind that fits them. Professor Boulding was not joking when he was talking about the need for scientists and others to understand the tropics. We have to find ways to fit their problems, not our problems transferred to them.

Yes, food aid must be part of a food policy and not simply of a farm policy as in the past. Even Food For Peace was not a food policy but a farm policy, since it was a surplus disposal measure. And it's quite true that much of the food that we gave away in large quantities was detrimental, strange as that may seem. Unfortunately, we were not concerned about where it went; we wanted to get rid of it so that it wouldn't depress our prices. Sometimes it proved to be a dis-incentive to farmers in other countries when we sent this food in at a cheaper price than the market, or at no price if it was under Title Two, and it would depress the price and force them out of farming. So we now know that you have to give food so that it isn't a dis-incentive to agricultural development. If you can give that food to the poorest people who cannot otherwise buy it, then it's not a dis-incentive and you are giving it to the right people.

We need a food policy, not just in the world, but in this

country as well. We have to look at all aspects of it, and we've never done that. We've looked at all the parts: farm subsidies, surplus food reserves, consumer prices, world food, overseas sales, Russians, Poles, embargoes, this and that. But we've never put it all together and said, "What's our domestic need, what are our foreign sales, what are our food aid needs, what are our consumers' needs, and where does that all come out?" If we have one great failing in our country, both in the Congress and in the Administration, perhaps even in the nation, it is that we are reluctant to plan. We are reluctant to look five or ten years ahead and we are reluctant to look at things as a whole. We tend to react all the time, rather than acting deliberately with a purpose.

I cannot let what Professor Barlett said go by without agreeing that even the Green Revolution with all of its hope has unfortunately helped the more well-to-do farmer who could afford fertilizer and new seeds. And of course many farmers cannot afford them. Our food aid, as she said, has to go to the poorest people. And you know that of the five million tons that we shipped this year, four million of it was sold on the open market, and only one million of it was given through the voluntary agencies. The poorest people do not have the money to buy food. I think we ought to go to a grant program. With these grant programs under Title Two, where we give the food, we have more control in the sense that voluntary agencies can deliver it, with less chance that it will be lost or blackmarketed or eaten by pests. For political reasons, quite frankly, Congress has always put most of the food aid in Title One, which is a loan program. So we give it to a country on a loan basis, then it belongs to them, is sold on the open market, and we have no more jurisdiction over it. It's supposedly only a loan, but then the loans are never repaid anyway; we get 18 percent of the loans back. I'm not saying that we ought to tell them exactly how to use it, but at least we should have some follow-through so that it gets to poor people. The food aid bill which I introduced tries to get a minimum level of food aid that is dependable—we say six million tons—and to use it for hungry people, not for political purposes. Insofar as there are any loans coming back, we specify that such repayments be used for agricultural development in the smallest farms in these countries, so that we increase their agricultural development.

It is very difficult to make sure that money given for food is used effectively. When food gets to another country there are all kinds of problems with storage and spoilage and pests. There are enormous problems of transportation, and black markets, corruption—the problems are absolutely unending. Now if we are not prepared to give up and say there's no hope, we have to find some way of participating in the real world even with all those adverse factors. My own judgment is that we cannot go in and tell them how to do it. First of all, we don't know. We don't know how to distribute their food best for them. We know relatively little about the uniqueness of their problems. In some areas we can give some assistance; in some areas we can give some direction. But I think we have to be very cautious about thinking that we know more about how to do things than the people in those countries do. So I guess I would come down on the side of trying to persuade and help and work with people rather than giving directives. I think they would receive an ultimatum in about the same way as we would.

I would say also that any attempt to tie population control to food aid must be done in a very unobtrusive way. I've just come back from a number of southern African countries where there is a combination of medical assistance, population control and food aid. I don't think you can say, "If you don't take the pill, you won't get any food." That's not the answer. But I think if we have medical centers and food centers or whatever, they can use these opportunities when people come in. In villages in Tanzania they have a medical center and a school and other basic facilities. When a woman comes in to have a baby in this kind of crude little clinic, which would be a few feet wide and a very basic type of building, you can talk with her about population control. Talking and making available isn't aways the final answer, but you can't force people into population control. You have to convince them into it. And they in effect have to convince themselves, based on their own economic situation.

PART TWO

RESOURCES AND GROWTH

8

Donella Meadows

Limits to Growth
Revisited

I have been asked to revisit *Limits to Growth*. I would like
to revisit it just enough to clear up a few of the misunderstand-
ings that seem to have arisen about the book and its message.
That will be, essentially, my analysis of what I think the world
is like now and how it is changing. Then I will go on to the
question, "Where do we go from here and how do we deal with
that kind of change?"

There are three important points in *Limits to Growth:*

1. The earth is finite. There is such a thing as a carrying
capacity, which is a physical limit to the number of people and
their paraphernalia that can be supported on the earth. The
carrying capacity is dynamic; it is not static. Technology can
increase the limits to human existence on the earth. We can get
more and more use out of fewer and fewer resources if we are
clever. The carrying capacity can also be decreased, by overuse,
misuse, short-term greedy use of the earth's resources. The carrying capacity is a dynamic system that is responding to the activities of the human population at the same time the population
is responding to it.

2. Population and capital on the earth are, at the moment,

growing exponentially. There are a lot of people who will argue about what these variables will do in the future, but there is no question that at this time both are growing exponentially at a considerably faster rate than ever before in human history. Exponential growth is by no means a new observation: Malthus was probably not even the first person to observe it, although he may have made the most noise about it. Virtually all populations grow exponentially when they grow at all, because of a basic fact of biology. It takes people to make more people. The number of people added to the population depends on the number of people who are already there. That means whenever populations grow, they grow exponentially, faster and faster. And they do grow, unless there is some limit, imposed either externally or internally, to prevent it.

Capital is dynamically similar to population—it also grows exponentially. By capital I mean the physical extensions of the human population: the tools, the buildings, the roads, the machines, the physical things that we use in order to extend our own powers and capacities. In fact, capital in the modern sense is a substitute for slaves. We now no longer use other human beings to carry out our wishes, do our laundry, or carry us about; we use machines and fossil-fuel energy.

It takes capital to make more capital. You need a machine to make a machine; the more machines you have, the more you can make; the more factories you have, the more new factories you can produce. Therefore capital grows exponentially just as population does, more this year than last year, and still more next year, unless some limit is imposed.

Another analogy between population and capital is that both of them, in order to be useful, require a continual input of energy and resources. Furthermore, capital, like population, continually emits pollutants. Capital takes up space, just like population. In terms of physical impact on the world, capital can be regarded as people-extensions. Therefore, if you are willing to believe that population growth might be a problem, you should also begin to think that capital growth might be a problem. Neither population nor capital can grow infinitely in a finite world.

On the one hand we have an exponentially-growing population of people and people-extensions. On the other hand there is a limit somewhere, moving up or down. The growth rate toward that limit is higher in some places in the world than in others. Nevertheless, the basic problem is the same, it's just more urgent in some places than others. Somehow, sometime, growth of population and capital in this world will stop.

3. That is where the third point of *Limits to Growth* comes in. *How* will the growth of population and capital stop? The systems analyst would say that any moving thing can slowly ease up to its limit with a nice smooth adjustment, if it gets an instantaneous, nondelayed, accurate signal as to where it is with regard to that limit. If you are driving a car and there is a stop sign up ahead, you can make a nice smooth approach and stop right at it, if you have an immediate view of where you are and where the sign is (and, of course, if your brakes work). The important thing is that the signal be there and be uninterrupted. If there is a significant delay in your information about where the sign is or where your car is, or in your braking mechanism, the system is not in control and you may go beyond the stop sign.

The same thing is true with regard to the human population approaching the carrying capacity. If we know accurately where that end point is and where we are, and if we have a mechanism for stopping, our approach to the limit will be smooth and controlled and well adjusted. If there are delays, if it is very hard to see that limit, if we go out of our way to deny the signals as they come in, or if we cannot respond quickly, then we are likely to have problems. If there is a delay anywhere in the system, the likely behavior of the system is an overshoot; that is, the population may exceed the carrying capacity temporarily.

If you look for the control mechanisms that tell the human population where it is with regard to the limits, you find there aren't many signals at all. That is, we really do not know what the carrying capacity is. Some people think it is very close and some people think it is 3,000 years away. It makes quite a lot of difference which of these two viewpoints is right, but we cannot resolve the argument. We do not know; we have no clear signal. In fact, since it is a signal we do not especially want to get, few people are even looking for it.

Furthermore, our brakes work, but very slowly. There are delays in our response mechanisms. It takes a human population 70 years to stop growing from the moment each woman starts producing exactly her replacement number of children. When mercury gets into the water supply it may take 10 or 20 years for that mercury to find its way to the ocean, and up the food chain and into a tuna fish. The person spraying the mercury around or the factory putting it out will not know for 20 years what the results of that action are. In the meantime the mercury is building up in a long pipeline. When the signal becomes apparent that there is too much mercury in the ocean, there will be 20 more years of mercury pollution coming down the line. These are just two examples of physical and biological delays. I don't think we can do much about them.

Other delays are social. First it takes a population a long time to perceive a new situation. It takes measurements and discussions and media coverage before we make up our minds that something is really different. Even when we have perceived it, we fight over what to do about it. Then, if we come to a conclusion about what to do, it takes time to implement that conclusion. For instance, now, after five years of wrangling there are many people in the United States convinced that we have to develop some source of energy other than petroleum. But even if tomorrow the whole Congress and the whole administration were convinced of that fact, it would probably take 15, or more likely, 30 years to convert all of the United States' energy systems over to some other form of fuel. There are social delays simply in deciding what to do and then in getting it done.

So the human socio-economic system is experiencing exponential growth. A number of our deeply-held values, both reproductive and productive, favor exponential growth processes. The earth has limits somewhere, we don't know where they are, and we are doing things to move them both up and down. We have many built-in response delays. Even if we knew where the limits were it would take us a while to accommodate ourselves to them.

Furthermore, in a period of overshoot, our resource base erodes. The carrying capacity goes down very fast when we are beyond it, and ultimately it carries us down with it. You hear and read statements suggesting that such a process may already be beginning, at least in some parts of the world. We have to keep spraying those pesticides because we have all those people to feed. We have to grow grain this year—we can't let the land lie fallow, although we know that a fallow period is necessary to keep the nutrient level high. We have to pump that offshore oil, we can't reduce our energy consumption. We have to construct breeder reactors, because we must provide power for all these people and for all this capital. We know that the number of whales is going down, but we haven't paid off the capital investment in our whaling boats, so we're just going to get those last whales. The Scandinavian forest sector has now reached a clear limit to the number of trees that can be cut each year on a sustained-yield basis. Unfortunately, the capital investment in the forest industry hasn't been paid off and there is now a movement to allow overharvesting for "just 20 years."

My conclusion from all these observations is that the human

socio-economic system is inherently unstable. That is, overshoot and collapse is a possible outcome. And if you look at the system the way it is put together now—the values, the biological and physical constraints we have to live with, the political, economic and social systems that we have erected—that outcome seems to be not only possible, but highly probable. That is what the first four chapters of *Limits to Growth* were about. The message is important only in creating the sense of a need for change. An overshoot of the carrying capacity is not inevitable; it needn't happen. Obviously we wrote *Limits to Growth* in the hope that it wouldn't happen. But if we sit back and congratulate ourselves, if we do not work very hard toward changing our unstable social, economic and political structures, overshoot and collapse is very likely to happen.

The earth is finite. There will be an end to physical growth of population and capital on this planet—not an end to growth of ideas, progress, or anything immaterial, but an end to material growth. I would predict that the end to material growth will come within 50 years. It doesn't really matter when, because the very thought that it will happen, whether we want it to or not, is enough for us to begin asking questions. What would a nongrowing world be like? Could we plan it and try to design a sustainable system, rather than the unsustainable one we now have? If we decided to set the limits ourselves, rather than letting the natural system choose them and overshoot them, which limits would we prefer to live under?

A steady state of capital and population means an enormous change in most of our basic assumptions about the way the world is. We all were educated in a world of very rapid growth. In fact, we assume it in virtually every course we take, and in virtually every organization we belong to. What happens if we do not assume growth? I find that thinking about a nongrowing population and capital base doesn't stifle creative thought about future worlds; in fact, strangely enough, it releases us from a lot of ruts we thought we were in. A no-growth world is full of wonderful possibilities.

Clearly there will be new technologies in that world. Technology will not be dead, the difference will be a new underlying philosophy, a philosophy that says, "We want to get the most we can out of our resources and our energy, we don't want to squander them." We will have to use renewable resources, not nonrenewable ones. That means solar energy and all the things that come from solar energy, for example, wind, falling water, and wood. Recycling will be essential. There will be less waste and less pollution. It is probable that these new technologies will be decentralized, not centralized, simply because the renewable resources of the world are naturally decentralized. Decentralized technologies will mean new settlement patterns and less urbanization. Each community or region will probably consume more of what it produces and produce more of what it consumes.

The kinds of capital that we have nowadays may be considered silly, antiquated, and wasteful. Whole new concepts will have to come forth about human needs and all the ways they might be satisfied. Other ways to move people around besides the automobile; other ways to keep buildings comfortably heated and cooled; other ways clothing and food might be produced. A lot of these ideas are springing up now. The most exciting ones seem to be coming not from the well-funded research laboratories of the world but from ordinary people doing experiments in little ways—organic gardeners, handcraftsmen, people who tinker with windmills and solar water heaters. These people understand the philosophy of the equilibrium state and are trying to design the technology that goes with it.

We are certainly going to need new economic forms in a steady state world. The whole conflict between the capitalist and the socialist systems may look meaningless from the point of view of a nongrowing state, which may combine the best features of both of these systems with some entirely new ideas. There may be no stock market, there may be no national debt, there may be no interest rates. Economic cost may be figured on a different basis than man-hour cost, which is the only thing our current system efficiently minimizes. We are going to have to minimize inefficiency of other things besides human labor, including inefficiency of energy, of resources, of capital, and of the pollution absorption services provided by nature. These are new concepts, and it will require a new economic order to carry them out. The whole system of money and exchange and markets may change—and considering how the old system is working these days, a new one will be welcome.

The patterns of resolving social conflict will have to be very different when we can no longer let growth do it. We will have to say, "All right, this is the pie we have, and now we have to figure out who gets what share of it, and the one thing we can't do is expand it." How do you resolve human conflicts under those conditions? I do not think the answer is "From each according to his ability, to each according to his need" *or* "From each according to what the market will bear, to each according to his greed." Those are both very primitive distribution mechanisms. We can probably come up with something better. That's a problem that can keep social scientists busy for the next 50 years. The answers that are actually evolved could be either terrible or magnificent. They could be unfair, autocratic, rigid answers, or they could allow whole degrees of freedom that we do not even know exist, because we cannot imagine them in our constrained world of growth.

The everyday institutions—the family and the business and the educational institutions, and the way you work and the way you play—will be different in the steady-state world. Again, experiments are going on now. They are interesting, and I don't know whether they are leading in the right direction, but I look to them for at least a glimpse of some new directions that are open to us.

It may be that the nuclear family is not right, nor the old extended family. Something different may be right; some sort of communal arrangement, especially since there will not be many children. In my house there are six adults and one child. I hope there will be one or two more children. The child is not mine, and I will not have one of my own, but this way I can have children in my house and help them develop without adding to the world's population problem. The capital required per family in our house is one-third of the normal capital per family—one washing machine, one kitchen, one tractor for the farm instead of the three we would have if we were living on three different farms as nuclear families. That solution is right for me. It will not be the right solution for everyone, but there are lots of other possibilities and lots of other experiments going on.

Someday we may decide that higher education beginning at age 18 and ending at age 22 may not be the best use of a college. It may be that people need some mixture of formal and experiential education all the time, and, in fact, the kind of education people need from age 18 to 22 may not be the kind that colleges offer today. Perhaps 18-year-olds would be better off traveling around the world and all of us older folks should be studying Chaucer and Milton. The content of our education and our needs as educated humans may also be a lot different in a nongrowing equilibrium society.

Our work could be more human, more craftsmanlike, more dignified, more complete. Our play could be more creative and less consumptive. If we didn't have to respond continuously to the pressures of growth, we might have both the time and the resources to make these dreams come true.

These are ideas that are consistent with my vision of what the equilibrium state could be like. You may have better ideas.

The important thing is to question our institutions as they are and ask, "How *could* they be? What are they really for? Are they accomplishing that purpose? Are there other purposes that are important that aren't being accomplished? In a society where physical growth has stopped, would this institution, this way of doing things, make sense?"

I have been talking about large changes, and I believe that such changes are necessary to stabilize the system, to bring it under control. What can an ordinary college student, a college professor, a housewife, a businessman—who is not sitting at the seat of power and does not have extraordinary riches—do to anticipate and maybe even encourage these changes? It's very easy to say, "Nothing, because I'm just a little cipher, my vote is only one vote out of a hundred million." My own vision of social change has itself changed in the last five years. I used to think that our leaders know better than we do, that they are seeing ahead and are making the necessary decisions. Now I know that in fact they are the followers. If social changes occur, they begin in ordinary people's heads, in the way they act and work in their everyday lives. Then, sometime later, the "leaders" find out about it. The world will change only when we change ourselves.

Let us consider for a moment the role of education in the transition to a sustainable state, because education is one of the keys to changing yourself. What can you personally learn, what tools of knowledge do you need in order to better deal with the changes that are going to occur? I can think of three basic categories of these tools.

First come the tools of thinking and understanding. You need logic, you need imagination, you need to question, to be able to process a lot of information, and to pick out the important parts. I think my science education was a great help in enabling me to deal with large amounts of information about complicated things. But what I did not learn, and what I do not see being taught nowadays, is how to put it all together, that is, how to get away from disciplinary boundaries and view the world as a whole system. Reductionist, scientific, disciplinary thinking is necessary, but in addition to that you need systems thinking. Specialized knowledge about narrowly-defined fields is most useful when you can put it together. The great thing about Garrett Hardin is that he is a biologist who understands economics, and the great thing about Kenneth Boulding is that he is an economist who understands biology. They can put it together, and that is what enables each of them to make a unique contribution to our understanding. That kind of thinking is very hard to learn, it is very hard to teach, it is very important to have, and it doesn't fit very well into the current structure of educational institutions. When you do have a systems understanding, you can begin to figure out two important things: where we are now, and where we *could* go from here. You can generate a number of possible future options and eliminate a number of impossible ones.

Second is a feeling for ethics, for philosophy, for social choice, for values. All that "soft stuff," which is what I called it when I was a hard-line scientist, is very important. It is the basis of everything you do, even science. I have read a great deal of philosophy since I left college, not because I was forced to by any liberal arts requirements, but because that was where I found answers to the questions I was asking. It is absolutely necessary to have that value-based viewpoint. It tells you where we *should* go from here. It helps you choose among the many options your systems skills have generated.

Third, one needs the ability to implement, to affect things, to be an agent of social change. The tools of thinking and of logic and of systems can tell you what could be, what is possible, how it all fits together. The tools of ethics and philosophy and values tell you what should be, where to go from here. But those two are very frustrating if you don't know the third thing: how you can make it so. That involves understanding how organizations work and how people work, understanding hierarchies, being able to communicate, to write and to read and to speak, to get your ideas into the minds of other people and other people's ideas into your mind. There needs to be more emphasis perhaps on what happens after the idea exchange—how people and institutions change or resist change, and how you can change them. If that sounds too manipulative, reflect for a moment on all the manipulative forces working the other direction—for growth instead of sustainability, for greed instead of equity. There is no choice about manipulating society. There is only a choice about which value systems will be more effective in manipulating.

If you do no more than change your own life, you have gone a long way toward avoiding what people call the "doom" scenarios of *Limits to Growth*. Once your own house is in order, if you have acquired the learning tools I just mentioned, you are equipped to work outside, to try to change others. You can start anywhere. There is no question of too soon or too late, too big or too small. If you are a college student, ask yourself, "What could be changed to make the college more consistent with the future steady-state world?" If you are in business, how can your business change? How could it anticipate and be on the leading edge of the steady state that will come. Being aware of these changes in advance can only be to your advantage. Wherever you are, how can you change the political scene, the advertising messages, the lessons in the classrooms, to reinforce the word "enough" rather than "more?"

One last question, the one that everybody asks: "Is there time?" Those who are more pessimistic than I am, and there are many, often say, "Changing institutions, education, even changing your own life—that's very slow. Social changes never happen quickly, and yet these exponential crises are coming on us faster and faster. Is there time to do all these marvelous things?" Well, I don't know the answer to that question. I used to ask it myself all the time, of course, because my whole life is dedicated to these changes. I try to get my students to dedicate their lives to these changes. It *would* be nice to know whether it's all in vain.

I don't think there is a guarantee that there is, or is not, enough time. In the absence of a guarantee, I have decided to stop asking the question. Designing and thinking about a new and better society than the one we have now is the most interesting, challenging thing that I can possibly think of doing. It is not a pessimistic, negative task, unless you are so much in love with this society that you can't imagine a better one. Searching for the equilibrium society is a very positive way to live. It can stretch your imagination and talents to the utmost. It can fill you with appreciation for the wonderful unrealized potential of our currently rather destructive species. Nobody's skills are inapplicable to the question, "What will the equilibrium state be like, and how do we get there from here?" Everybody has something to contribute, and a lot of imaginative people all over the world are already doing so.

Furthermore, to my own great surprise, I have found as I have made changes in my own life to be consistent with my vision of a sustainable society, each so-called sacrifice made my life so much better that I really don't believe I've given up anything at all. Rethinking my own priorities and reorganizing my life about the things that matter most to me has brought me a good life far superior to the overconsumptive one you see in the advertisements. That is disappointing if you like to think of yourself as a martyr, but on the other hand it means that life in a sustainable state is a good product, and it might sell. Even if there is not enough time to sell it to everyone, I can't think of anything I would rather share with my family and friends.

I once read a statement that made no sense to me at the time, but now I understand it. Martin Luther said, "Even if I knew that the world would end tomorrow, today I would plant a tree." Well, I don't think the world is going to end tomorrow. But whether I'm right or wrong, planting trees, sowing seeds for the long term, is exciting, enjoyable work. Today is a good day to plant a tree, to change our lives, to work toward a better society, based not on growth, but on sustainability. Those things are all worth doing in their own right, and who knows—our doing them may not only prevent the world from ending, but also make it a very beautiful world indeed.

9

Kenneth Boulding

Ian Barbour

Donella Meadows

Panel
on Resources and Growth

KENNETH BOULDING: All I have is a footnote to Donella Meadows' presentation with which I very thoroughly agree. Let me ask why technological solutions are popular, whereas ethical solutions are not. In the last thirty years we have just about halved the amount of poverty in this country by any standard you like to take. We have done this without any redistribution at all; we have all become richer. Per capita incomes have about doubled, so the poor are twice as rich, the middle class is twice as rich, and the rich are twice as rich. And we like this. We are making considerable progress in eliminating poverty without anybody sacrificing anything. That's the technological solution, you see. Now suppose in the next thirty years we do not increase per capita income much, which I think is quite likely. How can we halve poverty again?

Suppose that we take as an ideal for our society that we halve the amount of poverty in every generation. This seems like a reasonable political ideal. In this country the bottom 20 percent has about 5 percent of the income. If we want to halve this in the next generation, this means we have to transfer about $50 billion, at 1970 prices, from the top 80 percent to the bottom 20 percent. If we do this equally over all the incomes, this means we have to transfer about 5 percent of everybody else's income to the poor. The top 80 percent of American families now pay about 20 percent of their income in taxes. To obtain 5 percent more they would have to pay 25 percent of income, representing a 25 percent rise in taxes. This would include the carpenters and the plumbers and the professors and everybody else in the top 80 percent. Your taxes would have to be increased by a quarter in order to diminish poverty by a half, not to get rid of it. Some would say that all of the redistribution should come from the rich. The top 6 percent in this country has about 20 percent of the income, and they pay maybe 25 or 30 percent of their income in taxes. If you're going to get it out of them you would have to double their taxes, and they might not like that. You can see why these ethical solutions are not very popular, and why making everybody richer is so popular.

Now if you do this on the world scale it's even worse. The bottom 50 percent of the world population probably has an income under $200. If we're going to halve poverty in the world, this means taxing the rich, which in this case includes everybody in the United States. The poorest people in the United States are rich on the world scale, and this would mean taxing us an additional 15 percent of our income, or nearly doubling our taxes. Are you willing to double your taxes in order to halve world poverty? That's the ethical question if there is no growth. And that is why growth is so infernally popular.

IAN BARBOUR: I would like to raise first a question about the balance between concern for one's individual life pattern, which Donella Meadows expressed so movingly, and the need for national policy changes. I realize that she is not just saying, "Go to the commune to save your own life." Let us grant that changes starting from individuals and groups would provide examples of new social patterns that might become widespread. But the potentialities of decisions at the national level also require attention. When one looks at the developing nations it seems that their growth is absolutely essential. Third World countries think that any attempt to limit global growth would freeze them at their present levels, since they do not anticipate that rich countries will significantly reduce their high levels of consumption. I am more hopeful than *Limits to Growth* that improvements in mineral extraction, pollution abatement and recycling technologies can permit substantial industrial growth, especially in developing nations, without excessive environmental damage.

Of course, there are various kinds of growth. There is the intermediate technology which E. F. Schumacher describes in *Small Is Beautiful*. Western technology has been capital intensive, resource intensive and labor saving, and that is just the wrong prescription for most of the world. Only two percent of the world's research and development funds are specifically directed to the problems of agriculture and industry in developing countries. Moreover, most technology tends to increase the gap between rich and poor countries, and it often leads to the concentration of power. That is one reason why I strongly support Donella Meadows' enthusiasm for solar rather than nuclear energy. Maybe we need both in the short-term, but in the long-term solar energy is by its nature more decentralized; and it offers a type of technology which might be more adaptable to Third World countries. Yet we have spent on solar energy research only a very small fraction of the funds that have gone into nuclear research.

I am asking, then, how a global perspective can be institutionalized. Perhaps we must start with individuals, but don't we also need to work for changes in the structures of power? I do not see the rich countries moving very far voluntarily to-

wards changing their consumption patterns. Maybe the appeal
of new life patterns will have an influence, but this would take
some time. Perhaps only after catastrophes become more evident will people wake up. The price rises that OPEC has imposed on oil will occur with other natural resources as producing
countries realize that they have a new power arising from scarcities. It seems to me that changes will come partly by new
awareness in individuals, partly by new national policies, and
partly by new structures of power in the world as the resource-
producing countries realize that not only oil, but also aluminum, copper, and other materials have been coming into our
lifeboat from other nations. Perhaps a combination of such
pressures can cause a reordering of priorities as individuals and
as a nation.

My second question concerns the political implications of an
equilibrium society. Our democratic processes are geared to
short-range results. It is hard for a senator to look beyond six
years, or a president beyond four; any policy whose goal is
twenty-five years off does not have much political payoff. The
constituency for any election is limited in space as well as time;
people in India do not elect an American president, though
his decisions influence their lives. Now the authors of *Limits to
Growth* did not discuss its political implications. But many
people who read the book concluded that only a totalitarian or
at least an authoritarian government could possibly do the long-
range planning and impose the controls on growth that are
proposed there. I was therefore greatly impressed by Donella
Meadows' decentralist emphasis, though I am not clear to what
extent one could expect a regional area like New England to
be self-sufficient. Yet I still feel some tension between democratic participation and the demands of long-range global
planning.

I have some doubts also about whether a no-growth society
will automatically take problems of social justice and redistri-

bution more seriously. As Kenneth Boulding said, the poor have benefited from a general improvement of standards of living, without the rich having to give up anything and without any change in the relative shares. As the pie grew larger, even the person with the smallest slice received more. But with a steady-state economy only redistribution can benefit the poor. It is possible that in an equilibrium world the rich would hang on to their privileges more tightly than ever, and that social unrest and violence would be greater, unless there were some far-reaching value changes, including a greater dedication to social justice.

The kind of vision of alternative life-styles that Donella Meadows has held up is tremendously important. I find the redefinition of the good life that she has both described and exemplified very powerful. Some aspects of it are similar to features of earlier Christian ideals, although the new asceticism would not be mainly for the sake of spiritual goals but for the sake of other people and the quality of life which results. There are new ideals among young people on questions of desired family size, human relationships and the goals of one's own life, contrasting with the dominant values of an over-consumptive society. How can such value changes be extended and brought to bear on national decisions?

DONELLA MEADOWS: Let me make a comment first about the energy crisis as an example of resource scarcities. A lot of people would like to believe that the oil embargo was an accidental thing, a function of monopoly power which had nothing to do with real oil scarcity—and of course there is plenty of oil left in the world. But if we still had enough oil for our own needs in Texas, the Arabs wouldn't have the power they do. Oil reserves of the world are decreasing and oil needs are increasing. Because the rich countries have used their own oil first, and their iron, and their other resources, the poor countries are

where the resources are now to be found. It is a systematic result of the fact that the rich countries use vast amounts of resources and they start with the cheapest ones, nearest to home.
It has been said that the Arabs did us a favor by increasing oil
prices, and I think that is true. For one thing, higher oil prices
will spur the kind of alternate technologies that are needed.
If President Ford were really thinking in the long term he
would slap an import tax of $20 a barrel on oil. That would
encourage the development of coal, solar energy, wind energy,
and conservation measures. The problem with energy, particularly in the United States in the last twenty years, is that it has
been too cheap, not that it has been too expensive. The sooner
it gets expensive, the sooner we will get onto a reasonable,
long-range energy policy.

One of the results of using a computer model is that you
become aware of the interdependence of problems. I was at a
conference recently which dealt only with food. Looking at
food alone, the world's experts agreed that we could feed bil-
lions more people. All that you have to do is assume that all of
the world's energy, resources, capital and labor are put into
the agricultural sector. But the United States in the next 20
years is going to have to put half of its gross capital formation
into the energy industry just to maintain our current per capita
energy consumption. That conflict between agriculture and energy alone—quite apart from new pollution control equipment,
or the new houses and schools we would like—is enough to
make you wonder how much more growth is possible.

Now what about the question of a decentralist versus a global
approach to the equilibrium state? What is the best way to
organize social units? I cannot answer that question, and it's
one of the most burning ones in my own mind. I lean towards
decentralism, because I have read a lot of ecology and I am
impressed with the stability that comes from diversity. If the
whole world is dependent on the same oil pool in the Middle

East, our vulnerability on a global scale is very high. On the other hand, if some of us say "We're going to live on our own resources; we don't need that oil," then when the oil is gone, someone will have developed some alternatives. It really bothers me that the Eskimos in Northern Canada would have been able to survive an oil crisis fifteen years ago, but now they need oil to run their snowmobiles and heat their igloos, and they don't remember how to get along without it. That is a reduction of the stability of the system. So I intuitively favor decentralist, self-sufficient solutions—maybe not on the level of nations, but with some smaller boundaries than global ones.

I have spent much time in global conferences seeking agreement and not finding it, so I am also pessimistic about the very possibility of global solutions. On the other hand, global consciousness has got to be there. I suppose the best answer is some combination of globalism and decentralism, a global awareness and a local self-sufficiency. You try to get as many resources as you can from your local environment, and you know the reason for doing it is that you want to be less of a burden on the global scene. That is an ethic that holds together the local and global pictures. At the same time it allows individual diversity.

I don't know how you institute local self-sufficiency and global consciousness, because that involves a real change in values. I lived for a time in the Middle East, and in that society, as in most Muslim societies, a poor person will give someone who comes to his house half of his bread, even if it's the only bread he has and he has no hope of getting more in the future. He doesn't even think about that act, it is so deeply a part of the ethic of the society.

Today it seems to me that we need a similar ethic derived from global consciousness. You would never think of tossing your waste in the river, because someone down the stream is going to have to clean it up. You would never put sulfur dioxide in the air in Cleveland and Chicago, because you know that gives the rain in New Hampshire the same acidity as Coke. It hurts you to use an aerosol can because it means you would destroy some life-protecting ozone. How do people begin to feel that ethics? I know it is possible, because many people I know already live by it. I also know that a society based on the opposite set of values—local awareness and global resource dependency—cannot last very long.

I am grateful to Ian Barbour for raising the questions of whether in stopping growth you must freeze current inequalities, and whether growth should be allowed in the poor countries. If I could rewrite any one part of *Limits to Growth,* it would be the last chapter where I do say that stopping growth does not mean freezing income distribution, but I don't say it loudly enough. The people I talk to from the Third World never seem to have gotten to that chapter. I look forward to the end of growth because it will raise the distribution question so clearly that the rich people all over the world will no longer be able to ignore it or pass it off by saying, "Let them eat growth." For two reasons it's essential that redistribution be the cornerstone of the equilibrium state. One is the pragmatic reason that societies that have inequities are not stable. The value that I'm pursuing in seeking the equilibrium state is long-term stability. A situation where some people in the world eat ten times as much as other people, and those people on the bottom are starving, is not a stable state. It cannot last. It's not a desirable state either. Even if you like it that way because you're on the top, it won't last. That kind of inequity has to end, so there have to be varying rates of growth in the poor and the rich countries. Growth is not going to stop tomorrow in any case. The question of who should stop what kind of growth first is very important.

The second reason for redistribution in the equilibrium society has to do with global consciousness. I mentioned that as I have given up various material things my own internal happiness has increased. I think that is partly true because material things really aren't very important to happiness. But also, a person with a global consciousness cannot be happy consuming and consuming, if he knows that there are people starving. He can't sleep at night under those conditions. A lot of people in my area of New England are practicing what I would call voluntary poverty. They have adopted it consciously because they are happier that way; they can live with themselves again. Whether their renunciation of some material things does any good, whether it benefits the poor, I don't know. In our capitalist or socialist societies, material sacrifices probably don't provide help where it is needed. In an equilibrium state I think they would. But in any case, the knowledge that your lifestyle is not grossly wasteful compared to that of your fellow man makes you feel right inside. For both of those reasons—because I want the equilibrium state to be a stable one and because I want it to be a happy one—it cannot contain great inequity.

10

Rene' Dubos

Reasons for Hope

There are many reasons for taking a gloomy view of the future. I am as aware as other participants in this symposium that we have done great harm to our environment. I could give you a long list of horror stories, but I will mention only two. It has been calculated that if the present concentration of acids in the rain over New England were to be maintained for ten years, the productivity of forestry and agriculture would decrease by 10 percent. Such a decrease in photosynthesis would constitute for New England a loss corresponding to the energy output of fifteen 1,000 megawatt power plants. If you are not impressed about how bad the environmental threat is, please remember that figure. Few people realize how acidic the rain has become in many parts of the world, and especially in Scandinavia where such observations were first made.

The second horror story is about changes in climate. I participated recently in a congress in which world climatologists discussed what to expect of the climate in the near future, and they all seemed to agree that we are entering a small ice age. If the trends continue as they have since 1970, we can expect the loss of about 10 percent of the cereal production in Russia, 10 percent of the rice production in China, and a large percentage of the food production in Canada. And if that happens, it would be by far the largest single threat to food production in the world that we have ever considered.

My point in presenting such figures is to assure you that I am completely aware of the problems of the world. In fact, I believe I had begun talking about them long before most people did. And yet my manuscript is entitled "Reasons for Hope." If I present to you the facts that make me feel that the situation for the future is nowhere as bad as it has been depicted, it is not because I do not know the problems. I know all of them, I believe, and I can add to those which have been discussed already. Let me go directly, then, to the reasons for hope.

I am irritated by the title of the book, *Limits to Growth,* because I think it implies that growth means only quantitative growth, or that growth means that we will continue doing more and more of the same things we have been doing for the past hundred years. But growth for human beings is not only quantitative. The most interesting aspects of growth are quali-tative—how we change the world and how we change our-selves. And to this there is no limit. Are we not intelligent enough to conceive that there can be growth other than build-ing more automobiles and higher skyscrapers? I am going to plead that if you accept that there are all sorts of other ways of growing, qualitatively, then you will realize that there are no limits to growth because there are no limits to the range of possibilities that are open to the human imagination.

Let me begin by summarizing how I came first to be con-vinced that the so-called limits are not real limits. Most of you know of the book, *Future Shock.* It is one of those books that anybody knows, but nobody reads. It suggests that with all the technological and biological developments taking place, people will be faced within 10-15 years with new situations to which they will not be able to adapt. Future shock is the kind of culture shock that you will experience when all those extraordinary new technologies come into being.

I read the book when it first appeared. More recently I was in Paris and my French publisher had just published the translation under the very imaginative title, *Le Choc du Future*. There I was in a pleasant apartment in Paris reading it in another language and trying to see what it really means to people in an American community. It suddenly came to me that all those very complicated technologies which Alvin Toffler describes, whether mechanical, chemical, or biological, are technologies that have a scientific interest but are not going to change any of your individual lives. Your individual lives are still going to be made chiefly of loving or hating people, eating something that you like or dislike, taking every hour of the day and trying to make something as interesting as possible out of it. That supposed future shock is something that certainly will not happen, and it will not happen for a very special reason. Everybody in the world has now been conditioned to the fact that if we completely dehumanize life it would be horrible. Nobody wants it, and nobody will accept it. Without knowing it, you are beginning to reject in your own individual lives all those threats that are implied in *Future Shock*.

Let me give you another example, genetic engineering. You probably do not know exactly what it means, and I want to assure you that professional biologists do not know much more than you do. But on the whole it is something like this: that you can modify the genetic constitutions of people, or create babies in a test tube, or completely change the biological structure of the human species. Or it means that you can condition the behavior of people through all sorts of operant conditioning, or this or that kind of brain surgery. Now if you read all of this, it is absolutely frightening.

But let me tell you what is really happening. None of those techniques has been worked out. In fact, I suspect there are inherent difficulties that would make it impossible to apply them on a population scale. But even though they have not been developed, there have grown up all around the country an enormous number of groups concerned with the ethics of genetic engineering—the legal aspects of it as well as the medical aspects of it. In reality, society has already prepared itself for the threats of genetic engineering and of behavior control even before the events have happened.

In a peculiar way this is also what is happening with regard to *Limits to Growth*. The book maintains that if present trends continue we are going to have too many people on earth, we are going to run short of food, we are going to run short of essential supplies, and we are going to pollute ourselves with all kinds of industrial pollutants. Because this has been stated—in fact, it had all been stated long before the book, and had been a topic of conversation by those of us involved with environmental problems for the past 25 years—because this has been stated, a multiplicity of steps have already been taken in all phases of life all over the industrialized world to see that those projections of present trends into the future will not happen.

We live today in a situation in which we have developed not only the means of affecting the course of events through technologies and biological changes, but in which we have also developed the science of predicting the consequences of those technologies. Now this, I venture to say, is something entirely new in the history of mankind. When the automobile was introduced, nobody questioned what would be the long-range consequences of developing the automobile industry. When the industrial revolution began no one asked what would be the long-range effects of the industrial revolution on the lives of people or on the environments in which they function. This concern with the future, this projection of the present into the future, is a development which is not more than 20 years old and which, in fact, is only reaching its full expression during the past 5 or 10 years. And I have no doubt that even now the ability to predict the long-range consequences of our actions has begun to influence very profoundly not only the decisions of government but even your individual behavior, and much more rapidly than anybody would have believed. I could give you many examples, but I am going to limit myself to two.

An immense amount of money and engineering imagination was used in the development of the supersonic transport plane, the SST. But five or six years ago there began to be an enormous agitation among people all over the world as to the potential dangers of the SST. And even though we knew how to build a supersonic transport, the project was killed in Congress. Now I consider that a landmark in the history of mankind, when for the first time a technological possibility had been rejected not because of technological difficulties but because of long-range consequences that were not even clearly established but that were sufficient to dictate a change in policy.

The second example sounds less convincing but is perhaps more interesting. It concerns spray cans. You all have read about the possibility that the spray can may create atmospheric conditions which will destroy the ozone layer and increase, perhaps, the amount of ultraviolet radiation. This has not been proven, but the possible danger is there; some scientists believe it, and some do not. I am not going to take a position on the issue except to say that there are already countries that have ruled out spray cans. In this country spray cans have not been banned, but I have talked to some of the people in the industry who report that Americans have decreased the use of spray cans last year by some 20 percent—without any official regulation. I give you this as an example of the rapidity with which our societies, both at the official level and at the individual level, respond to the awareness that there is a possible threat for the future in some kind of technological operation.

Limits to Growth is based on the fundamental assumption that human activities of all kinds—human population, human technologies, pollution—are increasing at an exponential rate. Now I think one can say that exponential rates of growth exist only in the minds of mathematicians. There is nothing in the world that grows at an exponential rate. Any natural process, as it starts growing, calls into play all sorts of forces that prevent the continuance of the mechanism of growth. There would not be any possibility of ecological equilibrium in the world if this did not happen. So in nature there is absolutely no exponential growth. Things start exponentially, but through a feedback process various corrective mechanisms come into play so that the growth does not continue exponentially and some kind of equilibrium is reached.

The same thing happens in human situations. But in the human situation the control over growth also implies the fact that human beings never stand passively confronting any situation; before long they take some action to change the course of events. All of human history without exception is made up of those responses of human beings attempting to change the course of events. In many cases what human beings do is not wise; they have often made a situation worse by intervening. But what is certain is that there is no human situation that grows according to the exponential curve; human beings intervene to change the course of events. Wherever human beings are involved, trends are not destiny. And those of you who are interested in history can look at the history of any kind of social, technological, artistic, or even religious trend, and you will see that if a process is carried too far in one direction, automatically there is some kind of human response to it that changes the trend. So it is useless to use rates of exponential growth to try to predict what the future will be. It is almost an insult to human beings to assume that they will not try to change these events.

If you look at what is happening in our time you can find spectacular examples of how rapidly human attitudes and human responses change the course of events. Twenty years ago if one had made a survey among young women and asked, "How many children do you want?" the reply would have been 4.27, on the average. That was true in New York, that was true in San Francisco, that was true in England. Then around 15 years ago there began a tremendous amount of concern with over-population, concern that expressed itself in all sorts of books, all sorts of profound demographic studies, all sorts of projections into the future of what the consequences would be in this country and in Europe and in the rest of the world if the population were to continue to grow at that rate. And this type of concern was symbolized by a magnificent phrase, "the population bomb." Paul Ehrlich should get ten Nobel prizes for having invented that phrase, because everybody in the world became familiar with the idea of the population bomb.

How many children do young women want today? The surveys that were made in this country in 1974 showed an average of just below 2.1. I saw the surveys made in England, where the number is 1.7. In the Scandinavian countries it is below 2. In countries like Hungary and Rumania it is way below that, way below the replacement rate of the population. Even in countries that are reputed to be primarily Catholic like France and Italy, or certain parts of Holland and Belgium, the figure is just about the same, 2. You see that the public has been alerted, especially through a wonderful symbol that everybody can understand—the population bomb. The change within ten years implies a change in the most profound of all the human attributes, desires, aspirations, the love for children, problems of sexual impulses, any number of social considerations, traditions. In that most delicate of human situations, this change has taken place within ten years.

I have become so impressed with the rapidity of these social changes during the last few years that I try to make observations as to how such deeply held attitudes can change. I do not know any national or international figures, but among the people with whom I talk—admittedly a poor sample—the consumption of beef has enormously decreased. I am told that the farmers' organizations are getting to be very much worried that beef consumption has decreased. For what reason? Some people say it is because of the discussions about cholesterol; others say people are aware of the fact that to produce beef involves the waste of enormous amounts of calories.

I am going to take another example, the energy problem. It is not even ten years now that the general public has been alerted to the fact that there might be an energy shortage. A few technical people were aware of it before, but nobody would listen to them, and they themselves were not very convinced. About ten years ago some people began to worry a little about the fact that the supplies of petroleum in the world might not last more than 50 or 100 years. Then, of course, everybody became conscious of it at the time of the oil embargo in 1973, and people started talking about substitutes. At first, nuclear power seemed the answer, but it was found that supplies of uranium would be exhausted in 50 years.

Then the breeder reactor looked promising, and the technicians were convinced that this was the solution. All the technicians in this country, in Europe, in Asia, Africa, all over the world, were convinced that development of the breeder reactor would solve our energy problems. The federal government in this country established a phenomenal research program to accelerate the development of the breeder. In last year's budget, 95 percent of the research program on energy was devoted to its development. The official view was that the breeder reactor was the solution.

In the meantime a few of us became intensely worried about the potential dangers of the breeder program—mainly because, as you know, it implies the production of plutonium in enormous amounts. Plutonium is the most dangerous substance that has ever been handled by mankind, and there is no known way to store it safely. Several of us began writing articles about it, even people like me who do not pretend to have the kind of technological knowledge that understands all the principles of breeders. But I do understand that plutonium is being produced, that plutonium is the most dangerous substance, that there is no way that we know to store plutonium to protect the public against it, and that becoming involved in the breeder policy is therefore condemning future generations to live with plutonium. We began talking about it and eventually we succeeded in interesting a lay group of people in this project to such an extent that the National Council of Churches issued a report, chaired by Margaret Mead and myself, presenting to the public the danger of the breeder policy.

Whereas five years ago everybody was convinced that the breeder was the solution, as soon as people began to raise these issues, doubts arose in the minds of people in Congress and elsewhere in the government. In this year's budget for energy, instead of 95 percent being devoted to the breeder reactor, now a significant percentage of the funds is allocated to research in solar energy, geothermal energy, wind energy, energy from the tides and that kind of thing. Now the reason I am giving you this example is to see the fantastic rapidity with which our society responds to situations even of the most complex technological nature. And oddly enough it does not respond first through government activities. It all begins with you and me becoming interested in the problem, taking a stand, creating a climate of opinion, generating a general awareness in the public, so that eventually it reaches the mass media, and then only at that time government action takes place.

It seems to me that we are facing here an entirely new view of how our societies will deal with the future. Seemingly we are so complicated in our structures that it is impossible to change the forces of government. But in fact, if you operate through the channels that I have indicated, namely creating climates of opinion, getting people educated even though they do not understand all the scientific principles involved but are intelligent enough to see the potential dangers, then I think our societies can function much faster than they ever have in reversing those trends that they judge dangerous. And this is my fundamental reason for not being as alarmed about the future as some of my colleagues are. During the past ten years I have moved into the outside world, I have mixed with all sorts of people in all sorts of occupations—with politicians as well as men in the street—and I know that it is possible to so affect policies that the very concept of exponential growth becomes irrelevant.

I have to apologize for making this a very personal presentation, but at this stage of my life this is the only kind of service I can render. I am going to give another example that just comes to my mind to see how possible it is to change policies. New York's Kennedy Airport is adjacent to the largest bay on Long Island. Jamaica Bay is an extraordinary place, with an enormous amount of wildlife which used to be very spoiled because New York City used to dump its garbage there, but which eventually was salvaged through public effort. But a few years ago the decision was made to expand the runways of Kennedy Airport over Jamaica Bay adjacent to it. That is the most economical way to do it and technologically very easy. Some people began to protest because they wanted to save Jamaica Bay, but the technologists and the government in Albany decided that really this was such a practical solution that it had to be done.

But somehow or other an agitation began in New York City. We managed to talk to people who, without being in an official position, nevertheless reached influential people, and in particular we talked to the editors of *The Village Voice*—which was at that time an adventurous sort of underground paper. They began writing articles about Jamaica Bay, and because they had contact with television programs, managed to arrange a show at the Bay to illustrate for the public what it would mean if the runways of Kennedy were extended. Now in the meantime Governor Rockefeller asked the National Academy of Sciences to make a survey of what would be the dangers for Jamaica Bay from the expansion of the airport. Those of you who are familiar with such things know that such a survey by the Academy would be very well done, but the report would not come out for ten years, and by that time the runways would be built. So *Village Voice* arranged for CBS to send a crew to Jamaica Bay, and as soon as one knew that CBS would be there the *New York Times* was there too. I was asked to speak on the issue. What was important was not what I would be saying; what was important was that I would be speaking at a time when a big jet would be coming in, and a flock of wild birds would also be coming. And when that appeared on television with a picture in the *New York Times* the next day, Governor Rockefeller said that on the advice of his scientific advisors he had decided that the Kennedy runways should not be extended.

You may be alarmed about the clumsiness of our political structure, and I am as much as you are, but I wish to reassure you that in my experience—which is now a long one, and I could give you a long list of such things—it is on the whole very easy to reverse trends if you manage to make people aware, not of the scientific complexities of a problem, but of the consequences of a course of action. Here I am expressing a philosophy of public education that I have developed during the past few years. I used to be very much interested and took an active part in attempts at scientific education of the public. For example, I taught on science at the New School for Social Research, which tends to reach a large general public. I have been on television on purely scientific projects many times. While that still seems a desirable thing to do, I have come to see that this is really not the way to deal with such problems. Most of us are just too busy to take the time to study the physics of the plutonium problem, or to study biological engineering. But it does not take much effort to understand the consequences of a policy. So I have come to feel that we must learn to develop among people an awareness of the consequences of a technological trend. If we cultivate this approach, I believe we can make our institutions very rapidly responsive to all sorts of situations.

Now my friends in the Club of Rome say very justifiably that in many situations the trend develops so fast and the feedback is so slow that a dangerous situation—perhaps an irreversible situation—may be reached before proper corrective action can take place. They write in one of their most learned books, *The Dynamics of Growth in a Finite World:* "A system that possesses these three characteristics—rapid growth, environmental limits, and feedback delays—is inherently unstable. Because the rapid growth persists while the feedback signals that oppose it are delayed, the physical system can expand well beyond its ultimately sustainable limits, and the result is overshoot and decline."

Now I agree with all this. The point where I differ from them is that I have more faith than they have in the resiliency of biological systems, and in the resiliency of social systems. I think biological and social systems can take quite a beating and still recover if you give them half a chance. Concerning the resiliency of biological systems, I could give many examples. One would be Lake Washington in Seattle, which had been completely poisoned, not only by the domestic effluents of the city, but by all the industrial effluents. Some ten years ago citizens of Seattle began to agitate about it, and they managed to create a public policy committee and eventually convinced the city of Seattle to float a bond so as to restructure the disposal of domestic and industrial effluents. And within 7 or 8 years, Lake Washington had turned into a good lake, probably much better than it ever was before. Another example is the Hudson River, where within five years of public action the system had recovered. I was very much impressed; I had not expected that it would happen that fast.

Let me now, if you will, move to Greece. The Greek islands are essentially barren, with no trees. They have been ruined by erosion. And those of you who know Athens know that the nearby mountains are an immense barren area. But I have seen that if you take any area on these islands or on the mainland and just fence it, so as to prevent goats and rabbits from browsing, you find that spontaneously—without anybody doing anything or planting anything—plants start growing, and within 30 years you have an area of forest. You recreate the kind of ecological situation that Plato described 2000 years ago in one of his *Dialogues* as having been destroyed by deforestation.

Most of you have heard of the explosion of the volcano Krakatoa in the 1880s, the most enormous explosion of historical time. The island was split completely and one half destroyed; not only the island itself but the nearby islands were covered with a very thick layer of lava. Year after year, biologists have been surveying what has happened. And today the vegetation and even the fauna on Krakatoa island cannot be differentiated from that of neighboring islands. We know how it started, when lichens began to grow, then what kind of plant and what kind of bird landed there, and so forth. I know an immense range of situations where recovery has taken place even though everything had been destroyed. South of the Sahara an area of almost complete desert was fenced off to prevent grazing, and automatically vegetation started again.

I recognize, of course, that in many cases lots of people suffer at the time of destruction, and disaster can happen. If there had been people on Krakatoa they would have been killed, and for them it would have been a complete disaster. I'm not ignoring the disasters. What I want to plead is that if we look at natural situations, we can trust that there are in nature all sorts of forces for recreating something desirable. We can develop scientific knowledge about it, and administrative structures. We can help to create public opinion; we can show people what they can do instead of telling them to look at the bad things that might happen. If we give people not only confidence but knowledge that action can be taken, then we are much more likely to enlist the efforts of the public and official bodies in policies for the control of our environment.

I agree with Garrett Hardin that ecosystems are fragile, but I think that given half a chance they can recover. But it is true that in Nepal or the Amazon Valley, for example, one could do permanent damage. One of the reasons that Western Europe and this continent have been so successful economically is that we have had the luck to be living in the part of the world where the resiliency is the greatest. If our kind of civilization had been developed in the Amazon Valley or certain parts of Asia we would have created irreversible damage. I have wondered if technological civilization may have developed in temperate zones because recovery from damage is very rapid here.

I also think that social changes can occur much faster than we usually assume. There will be lots of crises, but we will respond to them. One hundred years ago Sweden was one of the poorest, most backward, agricultural economies in Europe. Within 50 years she became one of the most enterprising countries in the world, with the most advanced technologies—better than ours in some cases. Of course, there are all the human objections to technology, especially the mechanization of life, but in Sweden there have also been social advances. The Volvo auto plant was transformed so that instead of doing the same small task all through the day, a small group of people now make the whole car. The workers are not machines, but people who see their own products, and they are part of the governing body of their companies. So Sweden changed in 50 years from a backward agricultural nation to a sophisticated technological society in a human sort of way.

Concerning the concept of resources, I disagree with the Club of Rome in a very fundamental way. I would say that there are no natural resources in the world; all that we call "natural resources" are raw materials transformed by man. Let me give three examples. First, to say that agricultural land is a natural resource is to ignore the history of mankind. There has always been land in Minnesota, Western Europe, Israel, and Java, but it was completely unsuited to agricultural activities until it was transformed by human effort. Land in the Ohio Valley became agricultural because for two generations people cut down the trees and transformed forests into farms. All of Europe without exception is land that was made by man about 2000 years ago. Twenty-five hundred years ago Israel was a land of milk and honey, but it became unproductive desert land. But today you can see that within 25 years human beings have recreated the land, so Israel can now export some kinds of food. Our techniques for the production of food are still basically those developed in the Neolithic period; we use the same kinds of plants and animals that were domesticated at that time. But now it is possible to envisage some very new food production technologies. For example, increasing the amount of carbon dioxide in the atmosphere greatly increases the rate of photosynthesis; the trapping of solar energy by plant growth can be enormously accelerated. There are new kinds of agriculture without soil being attempted in several parts of the world.

Second, in relation to mineral resources also, a resource is not what is here, but what can be used by man for a certain goal. It is no accident that the first metals used in history were copper and gold, because they can be easily extracted, melted and manipulated to make objects. Iron came two or three thousand years later, because it needs a higher temperature for smelting and a more complicated technology. So while copper and gold have been resources for 5000 years, iron has been one only since the Iron Age when technology for it was developed. Aluminum has existed on earth since the beginning of time, but it did not become a resource until this century when a technique for chemical separation was developed.

Third, look at energy. In early history energy meant animal muscles. Then around the year 1000, men began to use water energy and wind energy, which was the real beginning of the technological revolution. New kinds of production, agriculture, and ways of life were introduced as water mills and wind mills became widespread. Wood was widely used as a source of energy for industrial purposes after 1600. The beginning of the Industrial Revolution was based on wood, and the first locomotives in the United States burned wood. The Industrial Revolution would have stopped dead if wood had been the only fuel, because it could not be replenished fast enough. Coal was then widely used—dating precisely from the time when the English forests were depleted, around 1780. By 1900, oil, which has existed in the earth since prehistoric time, became a natural resource because people learned to use petroleum products. Uranium became a resource only since World War II. So even in the case of energy, resources are being invented all the time. I expect to live long enough to see solar energy widely used; the main problem is storage. In the past 10 years a lot of scientific activity has gone into solar energy, and I have faith that within 10 years solar energy will be stored. That's where I have a profound philosophical difference with the Club of Rome; they assume that resources exist and are depleted, whereas I say resources are always invented.

I find that differences of opinion between scientists are seldom just differences concerning the facts, but arise from other kinds of judgments. In the debate about radiation between Pauling and Teller, there was agreement that increased radiation would be responsible for adding to the number of leukemia victims. But should it be accepted for the sake of national defense or increased energy production? Experts hardly ever disagree on actual facts, but they disagree in weighing the social consequences. Alvin Weinberg speaks of the breeder reactor as a Faustian bargain, and there is room for differences of opinion as to whether that gamble is worth taking or not. He has himself moved from unqualified support of the breeder reactor to a diversified approach to energy sources.

Finally, I think I differ by temperament from the Club of Rome. They consider that their main task is to warn people by depicting the disasters that are likely to happen if we continue as we are. I feel that the more important intellectual and practical task is to ask what we can do, to which they give little attention. Perhaps that is a reflection of my tendency as a scientist to transform any question into a positive one: what can we do?

I simply want to conclude by expressing my belief that, by engaging even more seriously than we have in some kind of prospective study of the future, our societies can overcome the myth of inevitability. And this is really where we are profoundly different from animals. Animals are prisoners of biological evolution. Once biological evolution has started in a certain trend there is no way that biological evolution can be reversed. Animal life is prisoner of biological evolution whereas human beings—all of us—are blessed with the freedom of social evolution, and social evolution is reversible. And it is for this reason that I want to leave with you as the final message, perhaps the final message of my life, that as far as human beings are concerned, trend is not destiny.

11

Kenneth Boulding

The Next 200 Years

I chose the title "The Next 200 Years," because, of course, this is a magic number. We are all thinking about the Bicentennial. Imagine yourself here in a time machine, going back 200 years. It would be very striking. The buildings would disappear, people would disappear, trees would encroach, a few Indians would be stalking through the woods. I suppose the carrying capacity of Minnesota 200 years ago was about 10,000 people, if that. The last 200 years have been a very remarkable period of human expansion, probably never to be repeated. We have an uneasy feeling that we are at a turning point, that in a sense one 200 years is over, and another 200 years which will be very different is beginning. Another reason why I selected 200 years rather than 50 or 100 is that I wanted to be optimistic, and it is a little hard to be optimistic about the next 100 years. I think we are going to have a pretty rough time in the world as a whole. I think one has to look beyond possible catastrophes to a larger future.

I had a very interesting experience a few years ago. I was being taken to an Indian market where there was a mosque. I have an insatiable curiosity, and so I took my shoes off and went in to see what was going on. There was a very interesting young man who had just returned from Mecca, and we got into a conversation, a most interesting ten minutes together. He described the extraordinary experience it had meant to him to take his pilgrimage to Mecca. Well, I want to ask the question: towards what are we making a pilgrimage?

There are really two kinds of valuations in human life. One is what you might call everyday or immediate valuation. I feel better off today than I did last Tuesday, because I had a bad cold and I was miserable. I am in much better shape today, so that my immediate valuation has improved. On the other hand, I know I'm five days nearer death. A pilgrimage value is a different kind of value. I was thinking of this in regard to the young man. If you go to Mecca, you start off perhaps from comfortable home surroundings, and you stay in miserable inns full of bedbugs, and you have storms and all sorts of things, and your immediate condition gets worse and worse all the time, but every day you are a day closer to Mecca. It is of enormous importance both for individuals and for the society to have a sense of pilgrimage. At the present moment it is very important for the human race as a whole to have a sense of pilgrimage, because we have become one world, and this has almost happened in my lifetime.

If we turn our time machine forward 200 years, what do we see? I think it quite probable that Minnesota will still be here. I am not quite sure about the United States, and I am not sure about automobiles. We are so addicted that we might have liquid hydrogen automobiles by that time—or we might have horses and buggies. There isn't anything more polluting than a horse, I might say; nobody ever produced a pollution-free horse. Still, that would just take us back to 1880; it wouldn't be all that reactionary. But I suspect we will have hydrogen-burning automobiles. Minneapolis may well have been destroyed and rebuilt by that time. I expect Northfield would look very much as it does now. Some things have a lot of persistence in societies like this which are stable and have a lot of fat. We have enormous quantities of reserves here. Bangladesh is about the same size as Iowa. Suppose Iowa had 77 million people instead of 2.8 million. Then it certainly wouldn't have any fat—any sort of reserves. So you look at the future and you see that the societies which have reserves may not be so terribly different from what they are now—just as the center of Oxford is not all that different from what it was 200 years ago. There are these great persistencies, particularly in societies with reserves.

On the other hand, the world as a whole may look very different. One thing I know about the future is that it is very uncertain. One of the greatest dangers of being in the prediction business is that people may believe you, which could be catastrophic. I think everybody who goes in for the future should have a label, "Believing in this man's predictions could be injurious to your health!" The further we go into the future, the more uncertain it is. And it is an irreducible uncertainty; anybody who thinks he can predict the future is either a fool or a liar. There is a nonexistence theorem about predicting the future, particularly of social systems. In social systems, knowledge is an absolutely indispensable element, and you cannot predict the future of knowledge or you would know it now. Knowledge is what is surprising, so there is an irreducible uncertainty about the future which mounts as you go on. If tomorrow is 99 percent certain, then 100 days from now is only 66 percent certain, and 1000 days from now is about 0.01 percent certain, or something like that. The uncertainty of the future increases rapidly as you go into the future in any detail, unless you have some kind of convergence.

But you can predict some things about social systems, particularly what I call the bathtubs. The bathtub theorem is a very fundamental theorem of the universe: if you add more to anything than you subtract from it, it will grow. And if you subtract more than you add, it will decline. Of course, the bathtub is a good example of this; if more water is coming in than is going out, then it will eventually overflow; whereas if you have more going out than there is coming in, the level will decline. Our oil reserves today are like that. One thing that we can be pretty sure of is that in 200 years the oil and the gas will be gone, even with the most optimistic expectations about new discoveries. There will still be a certain amount of coal. I'm afraid that where I come from is going to be the Saudi Arabia of the 21st century, as we have coal in almost unbelievable quantities—I suppose the largest reserve of fossil fuel in the world is in that part of the Rocky Mountain area. But even that will be running out in 200 years if we go on at the present rate.

So there are these various bathtubs that we know about. The pollution one is harder to estimate. If we add more pollution than we take out, it is going to increase, as it is doing in the world as a whole. Because I grew up in Liverpool, it is hard for me to be pessimistic about pollution. I feel that I have lived through a period of considerable improvement in the environment in a great many places, like Liverpool, Pittsburgh, and Chicago. I was in Chicago in the dust storms of '34 when Nebraska blew away and landed on the Midway. Now we know how to farm it a little better; we don't apply the European methods to Nebraska any more. We do learn how to do things a little better. Learning is really the key to the whole evolutionary process.

What kind of process are we facing in society in the next 200 years? It is not like celestial mechanics; that is a very bad model. I think the success of celestial mechanics was catastrophic for the other sciences, particularly for economics. The econometricians are trying to find the celestial mechanics of a nonexistent universe. It is not that sort of thing, and it does not have constant parameters. It is a little more like the growth of kittens and plants. We all know that a kitten, if it survives, will grow into a cat and never into a hippopotamus—a very fundamental principle. A kitten is a planned economy. It starts off with a genetic plan—very rigid, really—and the plan produces a kitten. Well, society is not terribly much like that, either, because as Robert Burns said, "The best-laid schemes o' mice an' men gang aft a-gley," whatever that is. Human plans always go wrong. There is a universal principle, Murphy's Law: "If anything can go wrong, it will." I was in Ireland a couple of years ago, and heard a corollary to that, called O'Toole's Law, which says that Murphy is an optimist.

When you are thinking about evolution, you have to think about Murphy's Law all the time, because you can state Murphy's Law in a quite unequivocal way, that if anything can go wrong, it eventually will. Evolution is a study of the highly improbable. That is why I think biology is not a science as economics is. It can't be a science, studying something that is absolutely ridiculous and improbable—four billion years of pilgrimage.

Look at a pair of glasses. They are the product of four billion years of evolution. You could not have had them in the solar system 400 years ago, or any time before that. Why? Because the solar system did not know enough to produce them. You could not have had the human race 10 million years ago. I do not know how old the human race is—it all depends on who was human, doesn't it? Ten million years is pretty safe; I am sure there was nothing you could really call human 10 million years ago. Why? Because nobody knew how to make us. That is, the genetic structure, which is the knowledge structure fundamentally, had not reached the point where it knew how to produce anything like us. So you have to see evolution as a process in the field of know-how, knowledge, and information. Know-how is what evolution is all about and what we are in for in the next 200 years.

The critical question is, "What are we going to learn?" This is the most significant limiting factor in the evolutionary process. At any one time what is around is limited by how far the learning process has proceeded. It may also be limited by materials and energy, because knowledge has to be coded into something. It can be coded in many different ways. If I am speaking, it starts as nerve patterns, goes out to you as air patterns, goes in your ear and gets translated again into nerve patterns. The substance of the universe is not matter, but information, essentially. That is what the universe is all about, right from the beginning. In a sense, helium knew more than hydrogen: it knew how to have two electrons instead of one. You can view the whole evolutionary process as a progress in knowledge. And knowledge is the improbable arrangement of anything that can be arranged.

Now, mediating the growth of knowledge is *encoding,* which is present in all processes of production. There are, as all economists know, three factors in production. But the three are not land, labor, and capital, which are not very useful categories. They are knowledge, energy, and materials. And all processes of production, whether the production of a chicken from an egg, or a building from the idea in the architect's head, or an automobile from a blueprint, follow very much the same pattern. They all start off with know-how, some kind of knowledge structure. This is able to capture energy and direct it toward the selection, transportation, and transformation of materials into improbable structures like you and me. If you put the elements in each of us down on the floor, it would take an awfully long time for them to arrange themselves into you and me. About four billion years! That is the essential encoding process, and, of course, it can be stopped by the absence of energy and materials.

The evolutionary process stopped on the moon some three and a half billion years ago; it got about as far as quartz, and did not go any further because of the absence of materials. It had plenty of energy—the moon has all the energy the earth does. But it did not have water, and it is hard to develop complexity without water. As you know, you and I are just water bags of the primeval oceans—with a little stiffening, physiologically. There is a good reason for this. It is hard to develop complexity in a gas because it is too radical. It is hard to develop complexity in a solid because it is too conservative. But a liquid is just right. Evolution is a ballet in water. It may be that we are the intermediary stage between liquid intelligence and solid, going on from transistors and computers. We may be just an intermediary; we may produce our evolutionary successor. I won't like it, because I have a very strong race prejudice; I am in favor of the human race. I am not at all keen on our successor, but I am pretty sure there will be one.

The human race is not the end of this process of increasing structure and increasing knowledge and increasing evolution, although I do not know, nor does anyone else, what is the "one far-off divine event, To which the whole creation moves," as Tennyson says at the end of *In Memoriam*. All that we know is that we are on a pilgrimage. I do not know what the optimum is. I do not know what the best is; in fact, I think that best is the enemy of the good. But I want to know what is better, which way is up. That is the critical question. As we look at the next 200 years, we ask ourselves which way is up, what is in line with the evolutionary process. I think one can give some tentative answers to this. I wouldn't be dogmatic, but I think there are obviously some things that we are looking for.

First, we are looking for a society which is more sustainable than this one. We all know that our existing high-level society, with our existing technology, is not sustainable. It has these bathtubs with big drains and no faucets. It has relied on easy sources of energy. Our whole society is here as a result of the fact that in 1859 we discovered an enormous treasure chest in the basement—in the form of gas and oil. And what do you do when you discover an enormous treasure chest? You live it up. That is what we have been doing. It is a little rough on one's posterity, but I have some sympathy with the man who said, "What has posterity ever done for me?" It surely does not have any votes, and all it has is our mildest sympathy and goodwill. I am just as deserving as posterity is, and I see no justice in sacrificing for posterity, any more than in sacrificing posterity for me. We are all equal.

But then the critical question is about the ongoing process of knowledge which is continuing evolution. Actually there have been times when I think evolution on earth almost came to an end. It was a very precarious thing. We are here today as the result of a series of very improbable accidents, and many times in the history of evolution things have gone wrong. But it survived because of this extraordinary capacity of the knowledge structure for adaptation, development, and mutation. But it could reach the limits of its capacity. There are things which could bring evolution to an end in this part of the universe. There is no guarantee that this process will go on. I must say, I hope it is going on somewhere else; I would not put all the universe's eggs in our basket. I suspect it is going on somewhere else, though we will probably never know just because of the sheer difficulties of communication. But we all have a prejudice in favor of its going on here, so we are in favor of sustainability.

Second, we are in favor of quality. We are not just interested in sustaining any old system. It is quite easy to have a low level of sustainability, like a village in India which has sustained itself in misery for 3,000 years. But I want something better than that; that is, I want a high level sustainability and a higher quality of life than in most primitive societies. And being an economist, I believe, up to a point, in being rich. I like being rich, and you like being rich. Let's be honest; we do not like being poor, especially really poor. Voluntary poverty is one thing, but involuntary poverty is extremely disagreeable. Even voluntary poverty can end up in that enormous cathedral in Assisi. You start off with poverty and you end up with great cathedrals and castles—it seems almost inevitable. Well, I like being rich.

Obviously you can be too rich, and perhaps we are too rich in this country. We could get along, certainly, with less than we do. On the other hand, our very riches give us a certain sustainability. It is easier to be sustainable when you are rich than when you are poor, because you have more redundancy. One of the great things that leads to survival in the animal world is this redundancy, this fooling around, as they say, like squirrels or ants. This is one of the great reasons for universities—the need for redundancy in society.

Third, there are some limits, and it is very important to know what they are. Population is one, and we all agree about this. The earth with 15 billion people is going to be very crowded. Survival and sustainability will certainly be much easier if we can hold it to what it is now or even reduce it. And reducing population is very difficult; nobody knows how to do it without catastrophe. There is not very much we can do about Bangladesh. Bangladesh with 10 million people instead of 77 million would be a fairly reasonable country and it could sustain a fairly decent standard. But how does one reduce a population without catastrophe? It is extraordinarily difficult; even war is not much good for reducing population. The only case I can think of where war really reduced the population was in Paraguay in 1870. That was the worst war of the last thousand years, and nobody has heard of it. But look at the Civil War in this country, or the First or Second World Wars; their effect on population was very small indeed, and there was recovery in a few years, perhaps a generation. Even after the Thirty Years' War, I suppose Germany recovered its population in 50 years.

It is this extraordinary reproductive power of species which enables them to recover from disasters. And when you cannot recover from disasters you become extinct, because there will be disasters—this is Murphy's Law. With any disaster which has a positive probability, if you wait long enough it will happen. Take a disaster with a 1 percent per annum chance of happening. In a period of 200 years it will have an 83 percent chance of happening, or something like that. I live in Boulder, and some time we will have a 100-year flood. We are going to lose a thousand people. Look at San Francisco, which is under an indeterminate sentence of death. Within the next 200 years it is almost certain to be destroyed. The San Andreas fault has not moved in over 70 years, and the tensions are rising. California has the absurd ambition to get to Alaska! Within X years there is going to be a major earthquake, and that is going to be rough on San Francisco.

The international system is like San Francisco—it has a San Andreas fault underneath it. That is what deterrence is—a system with a fault underneath, which has a positive probability of breaking down. There is a nonexistence theorem about stable deterrence; if deterrence were stable, it would cease to deter. There has to be a positive probability of the system's breaking down; it is about one percent per annum, I think. One percent per annum over 200 years becomes very uncomfortable. You cannot say when, but the probability of a nuclear war if the present international system continues is very high over the next 200 years, particularly now with nuclear proliferation. That is one of the faults under the system, and it is something we have to acknowledge and prepare for.

There is no law of nature which says that catastrophe will be avoided. Everyone that is here is a self-destructing machine. We all know that our genetic plan is that we will die—that is what the plan was in the fertilized egg that started us off. It is the same with the international system—that has a planned death also. This is very worrying, and certainly means that we must work on it; we must work on sustainability. How do you get a sustainable international system? How do you get a stable peace? How do you get a sustainable economic system? This means going to sustainable forms of energy, recycling materials, and population control.

How do you do this? We do not have the needed technology yet, but this is the pilgrimage; it is what we are working towards. There has to be a change in the structure of society. Or we might just learn to limit the catastrophe and put up with it. There are people who would rather live in San Francisco than anywhere else, even though they know that it will be destroyed. It will be rebuilt after it is destroyed, I am sure, because it is a very nice place to live. There are some catastrophes from which one can recover. Warsaw is an even more striking example; the Poles rebuilt it almost exactly as it had been before it was absolutely flattened in the Second World War. Munich and many German cities were also rebuilt almost exactly as they had been before.

There are catastrophes from which there is recovery, especially small catastrophes. What worries me is the irrecoverable catastrophe. That is why I am worried about the globalization of the world. If you only have one system, then if anything goes wrong, everything goes wrong. I have a lot of sympathy with Donella Meadows' concern for decentralization. I do not know how to do it, because it is very hard to overcome the enormous tendency toward uniformity. I was being driven into Nairobi a few years ago and I looked out at the skyline and said, "Good Lord, we've landed in Wichita by mistake!" Nairobi really looks very much like Wichita. And Singapore is beginning to look like Tulsa. Tokyo looks like London. It will probably be 25 years before Paris does. The only way of preserving any charm is economic stagnation. If there is development, then we increasingly get a single world, and that means we have to build up more defenses against things going wrong.

If we are to complete the pilgrimage, we must have social institutions that can put warnings at the cliffs. That is all I want, really. I don't want the optimum, and I do not know what it is. But I do want to avoid falling over the cliffs. In a sense, this was what morality was all about. Morality was a fence at the cliffs, wasn't it? You can do all sorts of things and get away with it, but there are some things you cannot get away with, and these are the ultimate limits, the things which would bring the evolutionary process to an end. It is enormously important to know where they are, and to defend ourselves against them. There are the obvious ones, like demographic catastrophe and nuclear war, but there are subtler ones also, such as unshakable tyranny which would suppress all mutation, all nonconformity. Evolution arises from a failure of replication; that is what mutation is, when the gene does not copy right, or when the student learns something the professor does not know, or when the children are not like their parents.

Finally, can you have a society which is rather stationary technologically, but which is not stationary in terms of the human spirit—in terms of art and literature, and so on? I don't know whether Donella Meadows' optimism on this is justified. One of the things I think we have learned in the 20th century is that socialism is very destructive of human creativity. In the arts and perhaps even in the sciences any kind of centralization of power can be very destructive of the creativity of a society (they also had lots of trouble in the sciences in the Soviet Union). We might produce a society in which we were so scared of change and nonconformity that we would suppress the creativity, the mutation that leads the evolutionary process.

We have to learn to put a high value on diversity and variety, and to rejoice in the fact that other people and other cultures are different. It would drive me up a wall to live in China, but

I am glad China exists, just as I am very glad the blue whale exists, although I do not want to be one. I would feel diminished if the blue whale disappeared, and I would feel diminished if the Catholic church disappeared, or Buddhism or even Marxism, because these are part of the total ecosystem of the world. They are part of the resources of the human race which we have to conserve. I am glad the Amish are still around; in 200 years we might need them. The problem of the preservation not only of the genetic structure, which is a very real problem in the next 200 years, but also of the social structure, is tremendously important. It leads to a rather different set of values —not that I am right and you are wrong, but that I am different and you are different, and isn't that nice? That can go too far, of course; I do not believe in preserving nonsense and I think the dinosaurs probably deserved what they got. I do not have any qualms about extinction; after all, there are a thousand extinct species for every extant one. Certainly nature has no qualms about extinction.

Well, I have not given you the answer; I do not know what it will be like in 200 years. Neither do you, and neither does anybody else. But vision we need, the vision of a pilgrimage to a better world. It is neither absurd nor sentimental to want a better world. And I can think of a lot better worlds than the one we have now.

12

Garrett Hardin
Roger Shinn
Kenneth Boulding

Panel
on the Human Future

GARRETT HARDIN: That was a very fine statement which pointed out some of our assumptions. One of the fundamental assumptions of the technological optimists is that whatever we can dream of we can have. I suppose most of us would deny the validity of that assumption. And, of course, one of the things we dream of is total happiness for everybody. But whoever said that God wanted us to be happy? We need to try new directions, but we can't forget the momentum of the past.

Suppose you see somebody jump off the Empire State Building, and standing at the bottom of the building are Boulding, Meadows and Hardin. Someone says, "Well, why don't you do something?" But what can you do when the person has jumped off? Of course, you could run forward and grab him and be smashed along with him; it wouldn't save him and it would destroy you. Whatever you want to do cannot be done for him; it's too late for that. Maybe this could have been prevented if you had encountered him a month earlier. If he had psychological problems and you had worked with him, you might have prevented it. And so with many of the things we're talking about, the catastrophes which we think are going to happen. There is too much momentum in the system to change it rapidly.

What we're trying to do is look beyond and see how we can prevent the next such suicidal gesture, ten, twenty, or thirty years later. What's going to happen in the near future is not inevitable in a simple deterministic sense, but for all human purposes it is practically determined. In the Second Report of the Club of Rome, Mesarovic and Pestel say that rich countries should transfer $250 billion to the developing countries in the next 25 years, or everything goes to pot. And they use this as a strong statement, trying to motivate us to do something. It is a sort of ultimatum: if you don't do it, then disaster will come.

But you cannot buy everything with money. I think if we gave the $250 billion that the authors of the Second Report call for, it would be wasted. We don't have the talent to do things such as to make people literate all over the world. How do you help a country like India with 600 million, 70 percent of whom are illiterate, with 14 major languages and a hundred dialects? Where are we going to get the teachers to turn them into literate people overnight? Again, an instance of momentum. So when somebody jumps off the Empire State Building, don't scold yourself if you failed to stand under him to try to catch him. Don't feel guilty; it's too late. Instead say, "Well, is that likely to happen a month or a year later, and can I prevent that?" And try to improve not tomorrow but perhaps the day after tomorrow.

ROGER SHINN: I find the panel a little bit too agreeable. It's not that we lack an optimist, who would be hard to find if he's thought about these problems, but we lack somebody who's really very uncomfortable. I think of conversations with a Brazilian urbanologist who's worried about the thousands of unemployed people herded in the slums of Rio and not knowing what to do. I think of a Nigerian physicist trying to introduce appropriate technologies into that society. Imagine in your mind what it must be to be an economist in India, trying to bring the intellectual tools of economic understanding to that social situation. I think of an army general and political leader in Indonesia trying to think through the energy problems of that society in the next couple of decades. No matter how much we may vibrate intellectually with those people, we are ourselves a little bit too comfortable.

Kenneth Boulding has said that the existing high-consumption society is not sustainable, but that there are sustainable alternatives. I'd like to hear a little more from him about how we get from here to there. Do we have to go through a number of catastrophes first? Is it possible to do some social planning to modify or soften the catastrophes? Does he see anywhere on the horizon political leadership that is really ready to deal with these questions? Boulding says that there are technologies of social change, social inventions, which I, too, think are very important. But there is a difference between physical technology, where you are manipulating materials that don't have decision-making powers, and social technologies—where you're always confronting the fact that the powerful people in the present system tend to be more concerned with preserving their power than with moving into a system which might be better but in which they might lose their power. This is why I have great difficulty with this question of how we get from here to there.

KENNETH BOULDING: There is a very profound difference between biological and social evolution. Biological evolution, while it isn't blind, is very nearsighted, whereas social evolution has a teleological element; it is guided by our images of the future. Our images of the future make a difference as to what that future is going to be. This is why I am stressing so much that we need to think about visions of the future, even if we aren't sure how to get there. If you don't know where you want to go, you are not going to worry about how to get there. Also I think there is probably a wider consensus on ultimate values, where we want to go, than there is on means. I've been struck by this in various seminars I have had with the Russians. When we talk about where we ultimately want to go, we are quite close. When we talk about how to get there, we are miles apart.

Anybody with any sensitivity is terribly worried about the present situation. We are quite obviously at some kind of a watershed in the history of the human race, and the past two hundred years will not be repeated. The world is full, and the whole period of the geographical expansion of the human race really has come to an end; with a few minor exceptions here and there, there aren't any great empty spaces anymore. This is a very fundamental watershed. We have to turn inward more.

The solution in the second Club of Rome report is rather unrealistic. One of the great difficulties is the problem of expanding the transfer of funds. In the 19th century the British exported about 3 percent of their GNP abroad in foreign investments. Now 3 percent of the American GNP would be $40 billion. But we have almost stopped investing abroad; thanks to the radicals, foreign investment has been completely de-legitimated. And gifts are likely to be small compared with investments. It is very rare that anybody got rich by begging, though occasionally people get rich by borrowing wisely. But now we have talked so much about all this wicked exploitation that we aren't supposed to do it anymore. This is why I sometimes feel the greatest enemies of the poor are their ostensible friends who destroy the only system that could help them. I know of no way back to the 19th century. The grants economy is slower and depends also on people's perceptions of the efficiency of grants—and we have quite legitimate doubts about this. So if we transfer $250 billion to the rest of the world, who has any confidence at all that it will result in wise investments? This raises Roger Shinn's question of the power structure, and that is a tough one. I have done a lot of thinking about this lately and I still don't know the answer. What is the relative role of struggle and production? The radicals are all for struggle; they are all Social Darwinists at heart. But in so many historical struggles it really would not have made much difference who won.

Roger Shinn asked whether it will take a catastrophe to initiate a sustainable society. The role of catastrophe in the whole evolutionary process is a puzzling one. The geologists aren't really quite sure how important past catastrophes have been. It is like trying to read a library that has burned down. The record of the past is so grotesquely distorted that our image of it is very dubious. The thing about catastrophes is that they upset the previous equilibrium. One of the interesting questions about evolution is why it didn't come to an end long ago—with the amoeba, for instance, which seems a very satisfactory form of life. One would expect that a system of natural selection would eventually produce a genetic equilibrium in which all mutations were adverse. It may be that natural catastrophes are part of the answer—magnetic reversals, tectonic movements, and so forth.

Social catastrophes have likewise been important. Look at Japan or Germany today and you see the advantages of catastrophe. Maybe the Great Depression from 1933 on did something positive for us; it cleaned out a lot of old firms, and off we went again. Ireland is an even better case; in 1846, it fell off the Empire State Building, as it were, picked itself up at the bottom, and never did it again; it really learned a lesson. But falling off the Empire State Building is a bad method of learning.

How do you develop the human imagination—so you can have these catastrophes in the imagination instead of in the flesh? Perhaps symbolic catastrophes could produce needed changes. The Meadows' scenario may have had such a function.

At Cholula in Mexico there is an enormous pyramid, cemented with blood from the Aztecs' human sacrifices. On top of the pyramid is a beautiful little Spanish church, all white and gold, where the symbolic sacrifice of the altar has replaced human sacrifice. How do you replace the real conflict of war by symbolic conflict which is less costly? I think that confrontation with symbolic catastrophes might help to avert real ones.

Editor's Note: In returning the edited transcript above with his revisions, Kenneth Boulding wrote:

"Oddly enough, the most interesting thing that happened to me at the Symposium occurred during the service on Sunday morning at which Roger Shinn spoke. In the procession we sang a hymn of Isaac Watts, which I am sure I have sung before without paying much attention to it, "I Sing the Mighty Power of God." I had an extraordinary sense of spiritual communion across the miles and the years with Isaac Watts, and I was greatly moved by him and by the feeling of the enormously long way that we have come from the serene personal order of Isaac Watts' universe. His hymn haunted me all the fall. I learned it and kept singing it to myself. I even produced a revised version, which I enclose. I must confess I would rather sing Isaac Watts' version."

I SING THE MIGHTY POWER OF GOD

I sing the mighty power of God
That made the mountains rise
That spread the flowing seas abroad,
And built the lofty skies.
I sing the wisdom that ordained
The sun to rule the day;
The moon shines full at his command
And all the stars obey.

I sing the goodness of the Lord
That filled the earth with food;
He formed the creatures with his word
And then pronounced them good.
Lord, how thy wonders are displayed,
Where e'er I turn my eye;
If I survey the ground I tread
Or gaze upon the sky.

There's not a plant or flower below
But makes thy glories known;
And clouds arise and tempests blow
By order from thy throne.
And all that borrows life from Thee
Is ever in thy care,
And everywhere that man can be
Thou, God, art present there.

Isaac Watts
1715

REVISED

What though the mountains are pushed up
By plate-tectonic lift,
And oceans lie within the cup
Made by the landmass drift.
The skies are but earth's airy skin
Rotation makes the day;
Sun, moon, and planets are akin,
And Kepler's Laws obey.

Is it the goodness of the Lord
That fills the earth with food?
Selection has the final word
And what survives is good.
And nature's patterns are displayed
To my observant eye,
The small by microscopes arrayed
By telescopes the sky.

There's not a plant or flower below
But DNA has grown;
And clouds arise and tempests blow
By laws as yet unknown.
However fragile life may be
'Tis in the system's care,
And everywhere that man can be
The Universe is there.

Kenneth E. Boulding
1975

13

Roger Shinn

The Wind
and the Whirlwind

*Set the trumpet to your lips, for a vulture is over the house of
the Lord, because they have broken my covenant and trans-
gressed my law.
They made kings, but not through me. They set up princes, but
without my knowledge. With their silver and gold they made
idols for their own destruction.
For they sow the wind and they shall reap the whirlwind. The
standing grain has no heads, it shall yield no meal; if it were
to yield, aliens would devour it.*

Hosea 8:1, 4, 7

We have been looking at the role of technology in the human
future. I suppose all of us have some perplexity about whether
this human race is capable of using its science and technology
creatively, or whether these will become our means of destruction. In some ways, the public worry about this has gone on
ever since World War II and the development of nuclear
weapons. In other ways it is more recent; only for the last ten
years has the notion of ecological crisis grasped the imagination
of very many people. And we begin to wonder, have we stirred
up a wind that is going to turn into a destructive whirlwind?

That language comes from the prophet Hosea. He looks out

at a greedy society where the powerful oppress the weak, where
people worship idols of silver and gold, where they think that
warriors and armaments and military alliances are the way to
security, where sexual love has been perverted into sexual exploitation, where lying, killing, stealing, and adultery are common. And Hosea says: this can't go on without destructive consequences. "They sow the wind, and they shall reap the whirlwind."

Hosea is talking about obvious forms of guilt, forms as familiar to us as to him. If we look at our own self-awareness we
might have to modify what he says. We might have to put a
little more emphasis on what you could call innocent perplexity.
The great steps we have taken as a human race to overcome
malaria and smallpox, for example, are not the result of our
guilt. These are among the best things we have done. Yet one
of their consequences is the population explosion that now in-
timidates us. That is what I mean by saying our troubles are not
all due to guilt. There is a kind of innocence in some of our
perplexity.

Hosea drops a hint later that maybe technology has something to do with all these troubles. He does not make much of
it, but he says life really was better back then when we were
living in tents. Now I do not particularly like that. Living in
tents is all right for a little fun, but day in, day out, I like solid
walls, plumbing, wiring, and all of that. As for the island
where I live, I would not know how to get one percent of the
people on Manhattan into tents. I like technology—but I am
concerned about its relation to our human goals.

And here we come to a religious and theological issue, the
complex relation between religion and science. It is said that
this is a history of warfare, and, of course, there are evidences
of that. Religions around the world have often cultivated the
life of the spirit, while science was dealing with matter—and
each was a little snobbish toward the other. Some religious

people did not like this materialistic concern. In Christianity, in particular, many of the church fathers despised science in words that embarrass us if we read them with any seriousness now. We all know Galileo had his troubles with the church. Even in this century we have had church-foisted inhibitions on the teaching of evolution; in fact, this argument is still going on in some parts of our country. If today the interference with scientific research is more oppressive in formally atheistic societies than in the more or less Christian ones, that only shows that any dogmatic orthodoxy with enough power is inclined to stifle new ideas, as the church has done.

And yet it is a curious historic fact that it was in Christendom that modern science and scientific technologies made their great breakthrough. To be sure, the greatest inventions of all came much earlier—the domestication of crops and animals, the invention of the wheel and the lever by unknown geniuses—but what we know as world-transforming scientific technology developed in Western Europe. A man named Hero in ancient Alexandria had invented a steam engine, but he did not know what to do with it except to amuse himself with it; it was a toy for the affluent. When a steam engine was developed in Western Europe, people knew what to do with it—and it was central in the industrial revolution.

Kenneth Boulding once put it this way, talking about the Benedictines of the sixth century: "Here for almost the first time in history we had intellectuals who worked with their hands, and who belonged to a religion which regarded the physical world as in some sense sacred and capable of enshrining goodness." And that, historians often say, had something to do with the growth of applied technology: people with gifts of the mind went to work to change their world.

Not many years ago, theologians were catching on to what historians were saying and trying to claim credit for this technological development. Nobody had paid much attention to theologians for awhile, but technology was a great success. So could not theologians get in on a little of that prestige by saying, "Yes, we really had something to do with all of this." So there was quite a sequence of books, the best known of which was Harvey Cox's *Secular City,* and all of them tended to exalt this technological achievement, this human ability to master the environment. Sometimes they even used such grandiose rhetoric as "the humanization of the universe." What that means to the Pleiades and Orion I never did quite know.

Now the point was not entirely wrong. It was entirely right in pointing to the ethical importance of decisions in technological areas. But it could not have come at a worse time for the theologians' purposes. Just as they tried to claim credit, people generally became aware that technology is dangerous, that it threatens to make the world uninhabitable. Albert Szent-Gyorgyi, himself a Nobel laureate in medicine, put it this way: "Science, with the powerful tools it gave us, made us outgrow our little globe. We can foul it, bury it in garbage, make cesspools out of the oceans, exhaust our resources, and wipe ourselves out." And Christian theology, which had been claiming credit for so much of this, suddenly found itself blamed.

In an essay which eventually became famous, Lynn White said: "The victory of Christianity over paganism was the greatest psychic revolution in the history of our culture." Today, even with all our secularization, the legacy still lingers. White wrote: "Epecially in its Western form, Christianity is the most anthropocentric religion the world has seen . . . By destroying pagan animism, Christianity made it possible to exploit nature in a mood of indifference to the feelings of natural objects." He concludes that for the ecological destructiveness of modern man "Christianity bears a huge burden of guilt."

The theologians, when they read that, did not know whether

to be pleased or disturbed. It was so long since anybody had thought they had done anything important that it was flattering to be told "You're responsible"—though they would rather have been responsible for something a little nicer. Whether White was right or wrong (and we could argue a long time about the details), he did point to a religious problem at the heart of our culture—not just a technological but a religious problem. If we have not been worshiping idols of silver and gold in the way the people of Hosea's time did, we have been doing it in our own way. We put our trust in the continuous growth of economic production, and expected that to solve most of our problems.

I want to read a couple of quotations from quite outside the church, and ask you to notice the language. From Dennis Gabor, the physicist: "Unfortunately all our drive and optimism are bound up with continuous growth; 'growth addiction' is the unwritten and unconfessed religion of our times." And from John Kenneth Galbraith: "That social progress is identical with a rising standard of living has the aspect of a faith."

Now if it is our religion, our faith, that has played us false, maybe we had better change it. And so we hear all kinds of calls for a conversion. Arnold Toynbee has blamed monotheism and urged return to something like a pre-monotheistic animism. I am inclined to think that is about the least likely of the possibilities before us, but when I see what is going on these days, it seems that anything is possible. Lynn White suggests a conversion to something like Franciscan Christianity.

Most recently Robert Heilbroner, an economist, has made an interesting proposal. He says the great symbolic figure of our cultural history has been Prometheus, the daring innovator, the ambitious achiever, the Titan who stole fire from the gods and made technology possible. We have about run out the possibilities of that mythology, says Heilbroner, and had better change our symbolic figure to Atlas, the burden-bearer, wearily enduring, patiently suffering under his load with no expectation of any dramatic success.

I have heard one proposal more radical than Heilbroner's. It has been offered by three economists, interestingly. The proposal is so radical that I can hardly imagine a theologian suggesting it. It is that we adopt the ethic of the Sermon on the Mount. I once wrote a little book on the Sermon on the Mount. As I look back on it, I realize that about half the book was an explanation of why we really cannot follow it, and the other half tried to show that we could make something of it. And so I was rather bowled over when this succession of economists—the first one to my knowledge was Kenneth Boulding in 1966, then Herman Daly, then E. F. Schumacher—all commended the Sermon on the Mount. Let me read just three sentences of Boulding. "In the spaceship Earth, we had better learn to love our enemies, or we will destroy each other . . . We will have to learn how to be meek, or we won't inherit the earth at all . . . We will have to learn how to be merciful, for we all have to live at each other's mercy."

Is anything like this possible? Before trying an answer, let me say something about how I think social change takes place.

Major social change requires pressure, especially pressure on the privileged who do not want to give up what they have. We have heard two United States presidents boast that our six percent of the world's population consume about a third of the world's energy, and that they wanted to keep it that way. We in the favored position are not likely to change in response to more exhortation or humble appeals from others.

But now the pressure is on. At a minimum we doubt that we have a sustainable system; maybe, worse than that, we are really headed toward catastrophe. I expect the pressures to continue. And, grim though it might sound, I almost hope for some mini-catastrophes that will serve as early warning signals and get us turned around before there is too big a catastrophe—

maybe a few more power blackouts such as we have experienced in areas of this country, some pollution crises, transportation difficulties. I expect there will be pressure in terms of making some hard choices: Would I rather pay the high cost of pollution (there is no way of avoiding paying for them) in medical bills or in restraints that make production more costly?

But pressure is not enough. Pressures alone can lead to a bitter, crabbed life where people are so insecure and up-tight that they refuse to make the very changes that might help them. Change, I suspect, is creative only if with the pressure there is some kind of vision, some quest for a kingdom of God and a kingdom of humanity. Then people not only have to change, they begin to want to change.

Neither pressure nor vision alone, I suppose, is enough. Consider as an example the racial changes in our country. Granted, they have not gone very far, and there has been a lot of trouble along the way, but some things have happened. Why? Many of us all our lives have known that racial discrimination was wrong, and we said so and did a few things about it, but we did not really do very much until there was pressure. On the other hand, pressure with no vision brought riots, clashes, bitter conflicts. When the change was most effective, wasn't it usually the combination of pressure and of vision?

This is the way the Old Testament prophets saw history. They pointed to these external events—the Syrians and the Assyrians and the Babylonians and the troubles of the society— and said, "Look what is happening. Don't you see in it elements of a judgment of God?" And then they responded with an appeal to conscience and a vision of God's intentions for his people.

What should the church be doing? I do not think the church has privileged access to any magical solutions or easy answers. What it can do is be alert to both the pressures and the visions.

Sometimes the church should become a pressure bloc in a situation of racial injustice or a struggle for peace. We will not often be one of the big pressure blocs, but we can ally ourselves with the pressures. But our distinctive vocation, what we are really here for, is to hold out the vision and then ask ourselves, "Can we not only talk about it, point to it, but begin in some ways to embody it in our own lives?"

Our future will require many a surrender of privilege, many a change in familiar life styles, but these threats, if we read them as the prophets do, may hide promises. Christians have always said that God's judgment, even when severe, is gracious, and when events show us that we cannot find happiness through extravagant consumption, maybe we will learn that there are better ways. I expect the learning to be painful, but it may also be joyful.

Margaret Mead said it well one day. She did it in a conversation, in her usual exuberant off-the-cuff way. Fortunately a tape recorder got it all: "Prayer does not use any artificial energy; it doesn't burn up any fossil fuel, it doesn't pollute. Neither does song, neither does love, neither does the dance."

That kind of belief comes out of a faith that looks neither to Prometheus nor to Atlas—though it might appreciate both those myth heroes—but to Jesus Christ. In him there is more of fun and delighted contemplation, more of fervor for justice, more of joy in sharing. He it was who taught us that man does not live by bread alone, yet it was he who fed the hungry multitudes, he whom we remember in the breaking of bread. Can we keep together those two insights, the importance of bread and the awareness that we do not live by bread alone?

My title is "The Wind and the Whirlwind." It reminds me that the wind can be benign, cleansing, useful. Our ancestors used it to drive ships and turn windmills, and now we once again may turn to it for energy. It makes the atmosphere livable after we have polluted it. Thank God for wind. But winds and whirlwinds can threaten; they can be fearsome, uncontrollable, destructive. "They sow the wind, and they shall reap the whirlwind." Is that happening to us? The decision is largely ours.

About the Authors

IAN BARBOUR is Professor of Religion and Director of the Program in Science, Ethics and Public Policy at Carleton College. He received a Ph.D. in physics from Chicago, and was chairman of the Physics Department at Kalamazoo College before graduate work in Religion at Yale. A recipient of Guggenheim and ACLS fellowships, he was Lilly Visiting Professor at Purdue during 1973-74. His most recent books are *Western Man and Environmental Ethics* and *Myths, Models and Paradigms*.

PEGGY BARLETT is Assistant Professor of Sociology and Anthropology at Carleton College. Her Ph.D. was awarded by Columbia University. She has done research in Costa Rica and Ecuador while on fellowships from the Ford Foundation and the National Institutes of Health. She has written articles on land use in Central America and problems of agriculture and economic development in Third World countries.

NORMAN BORLAUG received the Nobel Peace Prize in 1970 for his work in developing high-yield grains. He is head of the wheat program at the International Maize and Wheat

Improvement Center in Mexico City, and has written numerous scientific articles on plant genetics and on the Green Revolution. Many governments and scientific groups have honored him with awards for his contribution to the alleviation of world hunger. He has traveled widely as consultant on agricultural development in nations around the world, and spent several weeks in China recently with a group of U.S. agricultural experts.

KENNETH BOULDING is Professor of Economics at the University of Colorado and Director of the Program of Research on General Social and Economic Dynamics. He has been elected to the National Academy of Sciences and has held visiting professorships in Scotland, Jamaica, Japan, South Africa and several American universities. His writing is many-faceted, ranging from economic policy, price theory, and social analysis to religious meditation and poetry. Among his recent books are *Peace and the War Industry, Transfers in an Urbanized Economy,* and *Sonnets from the Interior Life and Other Autobiographical Verse.*

DICK CLARK is the senior U.S. Senator from Iowa. He completed course work for a doctorate in history at the University of Iowa, and from 1959 to 1964 was Assistant Professor of History and Political Science at Upper Iowa University. He was then administrative assistant to Congressman John Culver until his own election to the Senate in 1972. A member of the Senate Agriculture and Foreign Relations Committees, he was a delegate to the 1974 World Food Conference. He has introduced legislation requiring that U.S. food aid be used primarily for humanitarian rather than political purposes.

RENE DUBOS is Professor Emeritus at Rockefeller University in New York. A microbiologist and experimental pathologist, he was the first to demonstrate the feasibility of obtaining germ-fighting drugs from microbes, and he has done extensive work on the natural and acquired mechanisms of resistance to infection. For his scientific achievements he has received 18 national and international awards, and honorary degrees from universities throughout the world. Among his 19 books are *So Human an Animal*, which won the 1968 Pulitzer Prize, and most recently *A God Within* and *Beast or Angel*.

GARRETT HARDIN is Professor of Human Ecology at the University of California (Santa Barbara). Beginning in microbiology, he went on to work in genetics and evolution. He has written more than 150 articles and books, including the influential article, "The Tragedy of the Commons," *Nature and Man's Fate, Exploring New Ethics for Survival,* and several textbooks. His latest is *Mandatory Motherhood,* an argument against the right-to-life position on abortion. He has been a lifelong crusader for effective population control.

DONELLA MEADOWS, Carleton '63, received a doctorate in biophysics from Harvard. As a research associate in the Department of Nutrition at MIT, she taught courses on systems dynamics and population problems at both Harvard and MIT. With her husband Dennis she was an author of the widely discussed Club of Rome computer study, *Limits to Growth.* She has contributed to several scientific journals and is currently Assistant Professor of Environmental Studies at Dartmouth College.

MALCOLM PURVIS is Associate Professor of Agricultural Economics at the University of Minnesota. Educated at the University of London and Cornell University, he has worked extensively in Asia and Africa under U.S.A.I.D. and the Universities of Michigan and Minnesota. His publications deal with problems of agricultural development in Nigeria, Tunisia, India and Malaysia.

ROGER SHINN is Reinhold Niebuhr Professor of Social Ethics at Union Theological Seminary and Adjunct Professor of Religion at Columbia University. He has been active in the ecumenical movement, chairing several conferences of the World Council of Churches, and was a consultant on ethical issues in medical experimentation at the National Institutes of Health. He is the author of 13 books, of which the most recent are *Tangled World, Man: The New Humanism,* and *Wars and Rumors of Wars,* which won the Abingdon Book Award.

For Further Reading

* Asterisks indicate paperback editions

Barnet, Richard and Ronald Muller, *Global Reach: The Power of Multinational Corporations* (New York: Simon and Schuster, 1975).

Beckerman, Wilfred, *Two Cheers for the Affluent Society: A Spirited Defense of Economic Growth* (New York: St. Martin's, 1975).

*Berg, Alan, *The Nutrition Factor: Its Role in Development* (Brookings Institution, 1775 Massachusetts Avenue NW, Washington, D.C. 20036; 1973).

Berger, Peter, *Pyramids of Sacrifice* (New York: Basic Books, 1975).

*Borgstrom, Georg, *Focal Points: A Global Food Strategy* (New York: Macmillan, 1973).

*Borgstrom, Georg, *The Food/People Dilemma* (North Scituate, Mass.: Duxbury, 1974).

Borlaug, Norman, "Civilization's Future: A Call for International Granaries," *Bulletin of the Atomic Scientists,* October 1973, pp. 7-15.

Boulding, Kenneth, "The Shadow of the Stationary State" in M. Olson and H. Landsberg, eds., *The No-Growth Society* (New York: W. W. Norton, 1973).

Brown, Lester, "The World Food Prospects," *Science,* December 12, 1975, pp. 1053-1059.

*Brown, Lester, *In the Human Interest* (New York: W. W. Norton, 1974).

*Brown, Lester and Erik Eckholm, *By Bread Alone* (New York: Praeger, 1974).

*Brubaker, Sterling, *In Command of Tomorrow: Resource and Environmental Strategies for Americans* (Baltimore: Johns Hopkins Press for Resources for the Future, 1975).

*Byron, William, *Toward Stewardship: An Interim Ethic of Poverty, Pollution and Power* (New York: Paulist Press, 1975).

*Clark, Wilson, *Energy for Survival* (Garden City, N.Y.: Doubleday, 1974).

*Cole, H. S. D. et al, *Models of Doom: A Critique of Limits to Growth* (New York: Universe Books, 1973).

*Daly, Herman, ed., *Toward a Steady-State Economy* (San Francisco: W. H. Freeman, 1973).

*Dunne, George, *The Right to Development* (New York: Paulist Press, 1974).

*The Ecologist, *Blueprint for Survival* (New York: New American Library, 1972).

Falcon, Walter, "The Green Revolution: Generations of Problems," *American Journal of Agricultural Economics,* December, 1970.

Farvar, M. T. and J. P. Milton, eds., *The Careless Technology: Ecology and International Development* (Garden City, N.Y.: Doubleday, 1972).

*Freeman, D. et al, *A Time to Choose: America's Energy Future* (Cambridge, Mass.: Ballinger, 1974).

Griffin, Keith, *The Political Economy of Agrarian Revolution: An Essay on the Green Revolution* (Cambridge, Mass.: Harvard University Press, 1974).

*Hardin, Garrett, *Exploring New Ethics of Survival* (Baltimore: Penguin Books, 1973).

*Heilbroner, Robert, *An Inquiry into the Human Prospect* (New York: W. W. Norton, 1974).

*Howe, James W., ed., *U.S. and World Development: Agenda for Action, 1975* (New York: Praeger, 1975).

*Illich, Ivan, *Tools for Conviviality* (New York: Harper & Row, 1973).

*Kocher, James E., *Rural Development, Income Distribution, and Fertility Decline* (Bridgeport, Conn.: Key Book Service, 1973).

Lappe, Frances Moore, "Fantasies of Famine," *Harper's Magazine,* February 1975, pp. 51-54, 87-90.

*McNamara, Robert, *One Hundred Countries, Two Billion People: The Dimensions of Development* (New York: Praeger, 1973).

*Mayer, Jean, ed., *U.S. Nutrition Policies in the Seventies* (San Francisco: W. H. Freeman, 1973).

*Meadows, Donella et al, *Limits to Growth* (New York: New American Library, 1972).

*Mesarovic, M. and Pestel, E., *Mankind at the Turning Point: The Second Report of the Club of Rome* (New York: New American Library, 1974).

*Minear, Larry, *New Hope for the Hungry* (New York: Friendship Press, 1975).

*Myrdal, Gunnar, *The Challenge of World Poverty* (New York: Random House, 1971).

*Park, Charles, *Earthbound: Minerals, Energy and Man's Future* (San Francisco: Freeman, Cooper & Co., 1975).

Poleman, Thomas and Donald Freebairn, *Food, Population and Employment: The Impact of the Green Revolution* (New York: Praeger, 1973).

*Reining, Priscilla and Irene Tinker, eds., *Population: Dynamics, Ethics and Policy* (Washington, D.C.: American Association for the Advancement of Science, 1975).

*Rich, William, *Smaller Families Through Social and Economic Progress* (Overseas Development Council, 1717 Massachusetts Ave. NW, Washington, D.C. 20036; 1973).

*Schumacher, E. F., *Small Is Beautiful* (New York: Harper & Row, 1973).

Science, May 9, 1975 (entire issue on food).

Scientific American, Sept. 1974 (entire issue on population).

Shinn, Roger, "The Population Crisis: Exploring the Issues," *Christianity and Crisis,* August 5, 1974, pp. 170-175.

*Simon, Arthur, *Bread for the World* (Grand Rapids, Mich.: Eerdmans, 1975).

Soundings, Spring 1976 (issue on Lifeboat Ethics).

*Stivers, Robert L., *The Sustainable Society* (Philadelphia: Westminster, 1976).

*Ward, Barbara, *Rich Nations and Poor Nations* (New York: W. W. Norton, 1974).

*Ward, Barbara and Rene Dubos, *Only One Earth* (New York: W. W. Norton, 1972).

*Weintraub, Andrew et al, eds., *The Economic Growth Controversy* (White Plains, N.Y.: International Arts and Sciences Press, 1973).

FINITE RESOURCES AND THE HUMAN FUTURE STUDY GUIDE

"Finite Resources and the Human Future" does not pretend
to have all the answers to the problems it discusses; often
the contributors take opposing viewpoints on certain issues.
But it does identify problems arising from the increasing
demands an ever-growing population puts on this world's resources, and it provides factual information so we can assess
the seriousness of these problems. Though prospects presented are sobering, the contributors do offer some options
for improving the situation. Perhaps most important, they
offer hope that in spite of the immensity of the problems,
individuals can play significant roles in dealing with them.
There is something we can do.

This study guide is intended to help the reader identify
issues being presented and recognize how they affect us. It
will be especially useful when the book is discussed by
groups. Hopefully it may encourage active response by individuals and groups.

Group discussion can be enhanced by calling on people in
your community who could add information and viewpoints to

This study guide, prepared under the auspices of the Division for Life and Mission in the
Congregation and the Board of Publication of the American Lutheran Church, is to be used
with the book "Finite Resources and the Human Future," edited by Ian G. Barbour, Augsburg,
ISBN 0-8066-1526-5. Study guide © Augsburg Publishing House. Manufactured in U.S.A.

many of the issues: persons working in various world hunger
organizations, such as Bread for the World; organic farmers,
as well as modern big-scale farmers; county agricultural
agents; industry spokespersons; representatives of Planned
Parenthood or similar organizations; members of a commune.

1. Introduction

In the introduction the editor points out differing points
of view among contributors and poses some of the questions
they will discuss. It would be helpful to list these questions along with pro and con arguments as you come to them
in the book. See if you can develop your own perspective.

Concerns that surface repeatedly are:

1. Lifeboat ethics. What are arguments for withholding
material aid from some people in need? What weaknesses are
there in the arguments? Is there any happy medium? Note
Barbour's criticism of the lifeboat image and his alternative analogy of an ocean liner.

2. Standard of living. Is it realistic to expect people
voluntarily to lower their standard of living? If it is
accomplished by force, will the bad results outweigh the
good? What good does it do for individuals to lower their
own standard of living?

3. No growth. Can economic growth be halted without
causing overall depression or freezing present inequalities? Will a halt to growth result in more equal distribution or more selfishness? Might some kinds of growth serve
the same useful ends as our present emphasis on quantity?

4. Overpopulation. Is population growth best slowed by
economic development? Or is the matter too urgent to wait for
that? Should population control be a prerequisite for aid?

5. Government. Are democratic institutions adequate for
survival? Or are the measures needed possible only under
socialism, or even totalitarianism?

6. Environment. Can the perspectives of environmentalists
and those who want more for less-developed countries be
reconciled?

2. Lifeboat ethics

What does Hardin mean by "carrying capacity"? What are the results of exceeding it?

What is the significance of the fact that the biggest difference between rich and poor nations is the amount of energy they use?

What does Hardin mean by "limiting factors"? What limiting factors does he mention (p. 38)? If you had to choose among these, which would you prefer?

Can you think of any situation in which it would be desirable to limit freedoms--for example, the freedom to decide how many children to have?

Is "from each according to his abilities, to each according to his needs" a Christian point of view? Why is it not practical according to Hardin? Do you agree?

Make a list of your basic needs. Are the needs of people different in different societies?

Why is it impractical to send poor countries all the energy they need? How then can they be helped?

How does Hardin answer the question "How can you let them starve?" (p. 43)?

Do you agree that it is also pride that makes us think we can save the world from hunger? Can we do so?

3. Lifeboat ethics: a response

Who is in the best position to decide whether and what immediate sacrifices are needed for the benefit of the future?

How can we decide whether a present need or a potential future need is more important?

How can we cut down on energy use? What good will it do to cut down?

4. Panel on food and population

Do you agree that we should withhold aid unless birth-rates are lowered?

Has our aid to poor countries been counterproductive? Why?

What would be the consequences for ourselves if we turned our backs on those who need help?

Hardin says the time we buy is wasted (p. 61). Is it?

5. The fight against hunger

What can be done to put a stop to using the best crop land for urban development?

Urban consumers want increased production, reserves of food, and limited sales to other nations to keep prices down. Farmers fear overproduction or huge reserves because they tend to depress prices. How can the legitimate concerns of both be taken care of?

If it is impractical for American farmers to dispense with energy-intensive agriculture, is it reasonable to expect less-developed countries to get along with labor-intensive farming?

Some say if we used natural methods we would have fewer diseases and insects. What do you think of Borlaug's response (pp. 76-80)?

Note what has to be done to increase food production (pp. 80-82). What is the biggest hindrance?

Why does Borlaug argue against restricting meat consumption? What does he say is a better solution?

6. Food and development

Why is the world growing more interdependent?

Is it practical to talk about using money spent on armaments for food or energy development? Why?

Why don't arguments for birth control convince people in underdeveloped countries?

Do you think it is right to give food first to those countries who support our political stance? Why?

What legislation on food aid or development assistance could you support? Assign someone in your group to look up bills recently adopted or proposed in Congress. Are there bills about which you might write to your legislators?

7. Panel on food and development

What is wrong with sending a Minnesota-trained scientist to a tropical country? What should we do?

How can we distribute food to needy people without destroying their incentive to produce their own?

Why is birth control necessary in developed countries where there are no serious shortages?

8. Limits to growth revisited

Meadows says that continued expansion of capital is as much a problem as continuing population growth. What are her reasons? Do you agree with her? What implications does this have for the capitalistic system?

She predicts that material growth will cease in about 50 years. Do you think this is likely? What are advantages of no growth? What is necessary if it is to come about? Do you think it is possible to stop growth without beginning to die?

Our economy seems to be based on a need for continual expansion, with built-in waste. How can this be changed without causing an economic collapse? How can development be profitable but not wasteful?

What do you think of the decision of some couples not to have children? What will this do to the family as a basic social unit? What do you think of the commune as a replacement for the natural family? Should government use tax laws

to discourage having children? Who should decide how many
children are desirable?

Do you agree that changes begin with ordinary people, and
leaders follow? Give examples for your answer.

What do you think of Luther's answer to what he would do
if the world were to end tomorrow (p. 128)? How can you
apply that attitude in regard to the question of whether
there will be enough time to make necessary changes in our
world?

How can people be persuaded that giving up overconsumption
is not a sacrifice but an advantage? Do you believe that?
Why? How does it relate to Christian teaching such as Matt.
6:19-21, 25-33?

9. Panel on resources and growth

What is the difference between technological and ethical
solutions (p. 129)? Which are more necessary? Which are more
difficult? What ethical changes do you think appropriate?
Which are possible?

How realistic is it to expect people voluntarily to give
up their overabundance to help the poor? What are the prospects if they do not? Is there any way to accomplish sharing
without force?

Meadows says the Arabs did us a favor by increasing oil
prices. In what way? Do you agree?

If you can't be sure that your giving up certain things--
meat, appliances, fertilizer, etc.--will result in any
immediate benefit for poor people, why do it?

10. Reasons for hope

What other kinds of growth can there be besides quantitative?

Dubos says many predicted problems will not come about
because society when forewarned will prepare itself against
them. Do you agree? Give reasons.

How would you go about reversing a public trend? Do you think it is as easy as he says (p. 148)?

On what ground does Dubos argue against the "myth of inevitability"? What might the Christian concept of the creation of humans add to this?

Think of a recent environmental controversy. What environmental and social costs were at stake? What roles were played by scientists, citizens, courts, government officials, unions, industry, or special interest groups? Can you still study the issues and express your views at some point in the decision-making process?

11. The next 200 years

Do you think it is good or bad that we cannot foresee the future? Explain. What are your guesses as to the situation 200 years from now in regard to the matters discussed in this book?

Why is Boulding more optimistic about the long-range future than about the next 100 years? Do you agree with his expectations?

Boulding stresses the significance of learning. What have we learned in regard to the use of resources? Does this make you optimistic or pessimistic about the future?

Boulding indicates we are at an intermediate stage of evolution. How do you react to this?

In what way is "the best the enemy of the good" (p. 161)?

What do you think of his statement: "I see no justice in sacrificing for posterity" (p. 162)? What do we owe future generations? Can you relate our responsibility to the charge given in Gen. 1:28?

Give examples of "redundancy" (p. 163). How does this give hope for the future?

Why is Boulding concerned about centralization?

How does Christian hope relate to Boulding's position?

12. Panel on the human future

Hardin says it is too late (p. 169). Too late for what? Do you agree?

What does Shinn mean when he says no one is uncomfortable (pp. 169-170)? What's wrong with being comfortable?

Boulding says we need to think about the future. Take time to do this. What are your priorities for the future for yourself, your group, our nation? What problems do you want to avoid? What might be necessary to accomplish your goals? What can you do as an individual or as a group?

Boulding seems to say that investment is more likely to produce results than attempts to shift resources. Do you agree?

What kind of positive results do catastrophes bring?

13. The wind and the whirlwind

Sometimes good acts lead to bad results. For example, conquering disease leads to overpopulation. What do you make of that? Would we be better off without such developments?

How has Christianity contributed to the problem of exploitation of resources--and to its solution? What in Christian teaching gives the most helpful direction for the future?

Do you think these problems are a judgment of God on us? If so, what do you think God means us to learn from them?

In what situations, if any, should the church be a pressure bloc? What vision of the future should it hold up?

What does the example of Christ teach in regard to these problems?

In the face of the difficulties discussed in this book, what can be the basis for Christian optimism?